THE NEW TESTAMENT IN THE LIGHT OF MODERN RESEARCH

The New Testament in the Light of Modern Research

The Haskell Lectures, 1929

BY

ADOLF DEISSMANN

D.THEOL. (MARBURG)
D.D. (ABERDEEN, ST. ANDREWS, MANCHESTER, OXFORD)
LITT.D. (WOOSTER, OHIO)
Professor of Theology in the University of Berlin
*Member of the Archæological Institute of the German Reich
and of the Academy of Letters at Lund*

Wipf & Stock
PUBLISHERS
Eugene, Oregon

Wipf and Stock Publishers
199 W 8th Ave, Suite 3
Eugene, OR 97401

The New Testament in the Light of Modern Research
The Haskell Lectures, 1929
By Deissmann, Adolf
ISBN 13: 978-1-55635-454-0
ISBN 10: 1-55635-454-1
Publication date 5/1/2007
Previously published by Hodder and Stoughton, 1929

TO HIS DEAR FRIEND

DR. CHARLES S. MacFARLAND
GENERAL SECRETARY OF THE FEDERAL
COUNCIL OF THE CHURCHES OF
CHRIST IN AMERICA

A TOKEN OF GRATITUDE
FROM THE AUTHOR

PREFACE

EVEN at the beginning of 1927, by invitation of Oberlin College, I was to deliver the Haskell Lectures. But I fell sick of malaria at the close of November, 1926, after the conclusion of our first campaign of excavations at Ephesus, and was compelled to abandon my visit to America. Now I was favored, in the spring of 1929, to heed a renewed gracious invitation and to deliver the Haskell Lectures from April 10th to 17th in the First Church at Oberlin in English as here presented.

It is a pleasant duty for me now to express my grateful thanks to the Graduate School of Theology at Oberlin (Ohio) for their invitation and their kindly reception, especially to Dean T. W. Graham and President E. H. Wilkins. I consider the two weeks which I was privileged to spend in inspiring exchange with the faculty and students of the distinguished college an exquisite experience in my academic life.

The main credit for putting the text into English goes to my young friend Mr. Robert Hughes at Bangor (North Wales). To my esteemed fellow worker Professor Clarence Tucker Craig, Ph.D., D.D., at Oberlin I am greatly obliged for smoothing the English idiom of the manuscript for publication; he was also in other respects, during my sojourn at Oberlin, a devoted helper.

The lectures are printed in the present volume essentially as they were delivered. A German edition is for the present not planned, which was also the case with my Selly Oak Lectures.

ADOLF DEISSMANN.

On the Atlantic,
On board the North German Lloyd S.S. *Stuttgart*,
May 1, 1929.

CONTENTS

	PAGE
Preface	vii

LECTURE
I. THE ORIGIN OF THE NEW TESTAMENT (A)   1

II. THE ORIGIN OF THE NEW TESTAMENT (B)   39

III. THE LANGUAGE OF THE NEW TESTAMENT   71

IV. THE NEW TESTAMENT IN WORLD HISTORY   107

V. THE HISTORICAL VALUE OF THE NEW TESTAMENT   137

VI. THE RELIGIOUS VALUE OF THE NEW TESTAMENT   167

I

THE ORIGIN OF THE NEW TESTAMENT (A)

3

THE ORIGIN OF THE NEW
TESTAMENT (A)

I

THE ORIGIN OF THE NEW TESTAMENT (A)

THE Haskell Lectures, with which we shall be occupied during the next few days, are entitled *The New Testament in the Light of Modern Research*. Naturally, there will be an essential connection between all of the lectures.

First, we shall deal with the Origin of the New Testament. We shall seek to answer the questions how and when it happened that the individual parts of the New Testament were written, and how and when these separate parts, and only these, came to form a whole, a book, precisely the New Testament.

Then, having considered the Origin of the New Testament, we shall have prepared the way for the inquiry into the Language of the

New Testament. The interest in this subject is not confined to the specialist who has mastered the Greek language. It seems to me to be of great importance also for the wide circle of educated Christians, because modern scientific research into the language of the New Testament has produced results which have much more than a formal philological significance. They enable us to understand the native power and originality of the New Testament and, consequently, of Early Christianity, in quite a different way from that which was possible in former times. Already they have had considerable influence on the new attempts to translate the New Testament into present-day language. I may mention the English and American translations by Dr. Moffatt and Dr. Goodspeed.[1]

Then we shall speak about the New Testament in World History, reviewing the various

---

[1] Dr. Goodspeed, in the preface of his translation, lays stress upon this matter. But he inserted in his list of literature concerning the recent study of New Testament Greek some books which have nothing to do with it, and omitted books which by international scholarship are regarded as essential.

fortunes of the New Testament during its uniquely rich history through more than eighteen centuries down to the present day, a subject which hitherto has not been sufficiently investigated, but which, I believe, is among the most important for Christian practice.

With this we are brought face to face with a question which can never be raised with sufficient earnestness, a question which has quite a peculiar interest for the critical realism of the modern man—the question of the Value of the New Testament. We shall approach this question in two ways: firstly we shall inquire into the historical value of the New Testament, and secondly into its religious value.

The way in which I shall answer these questions is naturally determined by the peculiarity of my personal studies. The expositions are given to you as my own scientific conclusions and as such you may test and judge them. No one except the speaker is responsible for them, although many of the conclusions which

I shall give here are shared by others. The scientific investigator can never be satisfied with the mere repetition of the opinions of authorities. All respect is due to the authorities; without them we could have done nothing. But our ultimate purpose is not to ascertain the opinion of another about the truth, but rather to find the truth for ourselves as we see it. With our own eyes we will peer behind the curtain which veils the mysteries of the past.

This desire for the truth itself is the starting point of every real scientific investigation. Although this desire may often produce in us a just feeling of manly pride, it will ultimately make us humble and modest. Alone, on the steep slopes of the heights of knowledge, depending on no one, faced by the inevitable problems, we very soon perceive the limits of our horizon and the fallibility of our intellectual powers. In emphasizing personal responsibility for the conclusions there is also a confession of our own insufficiency and an admission of our liability to error.

Therefore, I do not wish you to receive my conclusions without criticism. It is also your task to see for yourselves.

* * *

I have just indicated that the characteristic features of my answer have been derived from my personal studies, and of these let me say a few words which will also serve at the beginning as a general preparation. The whole attitude of my studies of Early Christianity in general and toward the New Testament in particular receives its characteristic features from the fact that I endeavor to see them as clearly as possible from the background of their own age, that is, the early days of the Roman Empire, especially in the way in which that period has been made known to us by the archæological discoveries of the last decades. Whenever it is possible, I try to understand the age of the origin of the New Testament from its own monuments.

It was the impressions of my early youth in my Rhineland home which first drew my attention to the monuments of the Roman Empire. Through my father I first was introduced to those Roman antiquities of my homeland. Then as a pupil of the classical State-school at Wiesbaden, through the monuments which are there in the Museum like the Mithra-stone of Heddernheim, and through the excellent personal influence of teachers, I was filled with lasting love for antiquity.

Later, as a young scholar, I penetrated deeper into that amazing world of research, upon the entrance to which the Nineteenth Century has written a name in gold—the name of Theodore Mommsen. In close intercourse with pupils of Mommsen at Marburg and at Heidelberg, and soon working on the enigmatic monuments themselves, for fifteen years, at home in my study, I set myself to the task of endeavoring to understand the age of the origin of Christianity and the New Testament from its own relics.

Then in 1906 and later in 1909 I was able to make long journeys into Greece, Asia Minor,

Syria, Palestine, and Egypt in order to see, with my own eyes, the world in which the New Testament originated, the sunny wonder-world of the Near East.

Under the impressions of these travels I became more and more convinced of the importance of Asia Minor, and in particular of Ephesus, the capital of the Roman province of Asia, for the proper estimation of the letters of Paul and the writings of John. For that reason I have spent much time and strength during the last years in the attempt to revive archæological research in Asia Minor and especially the excavating work at Ephesus, which had come to a standstill during the war. The scholars of the Austrian Archæological Institute of Vienna had done excellent work in Ephesus before the war. One of the things that give me the greatest satisfaction is that in 1926 I succeeded in getting together a considerable fund for the work in Ephesus. Austria gave, in Professor Joseph Keil, a brilliant leader for the new excavating work. So we were able, in 1926, 1927, and 1928, to make three big and successful expeditions to Ephesus. These Ephesus days were of exceptional value to me. I could stay for many weeks on the site of the metropolis of Paul and John, and in that way enrich my mental picture of the eastern home of Christianity.

In consequence of these experiences and studies, when I undertake a scientific study of Early Christianity and the New Testament in their own age I must lay more emphasis than has generally been done in the past on the following points: first that of the history of culture, literary as well as unliterary; secondly, that of the history of language, and lastly that of cult history. This last expression, "cult history," may perhaps sound strange to some of you. The exact meaning of this technical word has been explained in the new edition of my book on Paul.[2]

* * *

---

[2] *Paul: A Study in Social and Religious History.* Second Edition, p. 114 ff.

THE ORIGIN

With what has already been said, I believe that the way is now prepared for us to travel together. Now I may undertake to guide you over the first stage of our journey. We shall seek to understand the Origin of the New Testament.

The inquiry into the Origins of the New Testament is a historical one, a problem for the science of history. It is a question concerning an event, a fact, which lies in the past: How did the New Testament originate?

Through the centuries the only answer to this question has been a religious one. The fathers of Protestant dogmatics have maintained a view of the Holy Scriptures in accordance with the teachings of the Rabbis, the Church Fathers, and the theologians of the Middle Ages, namely, that the New Testament came into existence through divine inspiration, that is, through divine suggestion. Or, still more definitely, the Spirit of God breathed the words of the New Testament into the Apostles as if the words were dictated to them. Just as a stenographer receiving letters from a business man works quite mechanically, so were the Apostles pens and pencils of the Holy Spirit. This dogma of verbal inspiration of every letter of the New Testament, which rightly can be called mechanical inspiration, is now abandoned in all scientific theology.

We cannot accept the religious answer which has been given to our historical question, that is, the answer given by the theory of verbal inspiration. Why do we reject it? We reject it, not because it is a religious answer, and not because it speaks of inspiration. There is such a thing as inspiration. There is artistic inspiration and poetic inspiration. And there is also prophetic inspiration. Without inspiration there would be no Christianity, and the New Testament would never have originated.

On the other hand, I could also give a religious answer to this historical question from the standpoint of my Christian belief in Divine Providence. By comparing the New Testament to a great church building I could say:

THE ORIGIN

We must thank the Master-Builder for this sanctuary. It was according to His plans that the Evangelists and the Apostles worked. The foundation which was laid by the Master-Builder Himself is the personality of Jesus and His eternal words. On this foundation the Apostles began the building work with massive, hewn stones. From the workshop of Paul came the living forest of aspiring columns, on which the dome of the Acts of the Apostles rests securely. The big windows with the crystal splendor of their richly colored paintings are the Revelation of John. The Fourth Gospel is the tower reaching upward, its open work allowing a part of the blue sky to glitter through. And the Epistles are the different toned but harmonious bells which ring to call together the people of the Lord.

That would be our own attempt to give a religious answer to this historical question. And because we have our own religious answer we respect and appreciate the religious motives underlying the old doctrine of inspiration.

We may say again, it is not because it is a religious answer that we reject the theory of verbal inspiration, nor because it speaks of inspiration, but rather because it conceives of inspiration as mechanical, and this mechanical conception eliminates what is best in the Evangelists and the Apostles, their individuality. It degrades Paul, John, and all the others into mere writing machines. In order to make the letter sacred, the old view deprived the Spirit of what makes him a Spirit.

But, further, our own religious answer which we have put in the place of the obsolete doctrine of inspiration is not a sufficient answer to the historical question. Historical questions demand historical answers. If I stand before a cathedral in a strange town and ask an old native: "Who built this cathedral?" and the old man answers solemnly: "We must thank God's good grace for this wonderful building," he has undoubtedly given me an answer to which there can be no objection, a good sensible answer. But he has not answered my historical question. I want to know something of the men who built the cathedral, its date, and further fortunes.

The question as to the origin of the New Testament has a similar meaning. It demands an historical answer, without disputing, in any way, the truth and the value of a religious answer.

* * *

The New Testament, as we have it, is a book, and it originated in an age which was full of books. The age of the Roman Empire is, in writings and books, one of the richest we know. And this wealth of the early Imperial period appears, above all, in the sphere of literature. It is true that all the literature of that period has not been preserved for us today. In the storms of the centuries much of it was blown away and lost forever. But what has been preserved justifies us in regarding, particularly the days of Augustus, as the Golden Age of Roman literature. It is the age of the poets, Horace, Virgil, Propertius, Tibullus, and Ovid, and of the historian Livy, and a series of other brilliant Latin authors, which comes to an end under the successors of Augustus. The Greek writings, which were produced in the early days of the Empire, are also significant, especially the scientific literature. Diodor of Sicily undertook a history of the world in forty volumes, Dionysius of Halicarnassus wrote a Roman history in twenty volumes, and Strabo published his magnificent geographical work in seventeen books.

But that is not all. Even more than what was written by men of literature was written by the officers of the Roman provinces and cities and in private life. We mentioned the men of literature first because it is their works which generally engage our attention. But if we wish to recognize the age of the origin of Christianity as an age rich in writing we must not forget the vast amount which was written at that time for the purpose of the state, law-giving, administration of justice,

THE ORIGIN

for military purposes, for social life in families and communities and in general trade.

That is to say, the official writing was, in proportion, no smaller than it is with us to-day. We have known this for a long time from the multitude of inscriptions belonging to that period. Laws, Imperial decrees, and treaties of state, and many other things used to be inscribed in stones, or cast in bronze, and the inscribed stones or tablets were stored in public places, in temples and state buildings. We have to thank these circumstances that we have such a significant remainder of the official writing preserved for us.

During the last decades other discoveries were added to the stone and bronze inscriptions, and these have given us a really startling glimpse of the extent of writing in the early Imperial days. In the ancient wonderland on the Nile, in Egypt, during the excavations among the ruins of ancient cities, places have been discovered where in olden times all kinds of worthless rubbish were thrown. In these refuse and rubbish heaps a great mass of Greek writings has been found, whose contents, when deciphered, proved to be of the most miscellaneous kind: lease and rent arrangements, bills and receipts, decrees issued by the authorities, proclamations, sentences of court, minutes of judicial proceedings, tax assessments, and many other things, especially private letters. Most of these fragments belong to the days of the Roman Empire. They were written upon the most durable materials, either on pieces of pottery—these are usually known by the Greek name *ostraca*—or on leaves of papyrus, the forerunner of our paper.

The papyri sheets were made in Egypt from the pith of the papyrus plant, and the durability of this writing material is proved by the fact that those leaves have been in Egyptian soil, without any further protection, for fifteen to sixteen centuries, some for three or four thousand years and more. When they were discovered part of them appeared quite fresh. The oldest written papyrus known to us dates

THE ORIGIN

from about two thousand six hundred years B. C., and is therefore about four thousand five hundred years old. In our soil and under our northern sky this would have been quite impossible. For the preservation of so many thousands of these time-honored texts we must thank, firstly, the dry Egyptian soil, which, under the blazing African sun, is in many parts never moistened by a shower, and, secondly, the indestructible nature of the papyrus sheets and potsherds upon which the texts are written. The papyri, which were formerly thrown into the refuse heaps as waste and rubbish, are to-day carefully packed between air-tight, cemented glass plates, the most costly treasures in our libraries and museums.

These Egyptian papyri discoveries offer a vast amount of new knowledge to the student of antiquity. For details, I may perhaps refer you to the studies which I have published in my book *Light from the Ancient East*.[3] A clear

---

[3] *Light from the Ancient East*. The New Testament illustrated by recently discovered texts of the Graeco-Roman World. New and completely revised edition, New York, 1927.

light is shed upon the life of the people in the ancient world, life in the villages and the small towns, in trade and travel, in matters of law and district administration. For our purpose we can learn through these discoveries of the great amount of writing which was done in the Roman Empire at the time of the rise of Christianity. Further, from the Egyptian discoveries we may draw conclusions about writing in other provinces of the Empire. We have hardly any papyri texts of that time from Asia Minor, Greece, Italy, Gaul, Spain, and the other provinces, but we have a great number of stone inscriptions.

Moreover, we learn, not only that there was a great deal of writing, but also that there was much reading. Among the Egyptian papyri texts are found remains of books, for example, Homer and other poets. In the Italian city, Herculaneum, which was buried by the terrible eruption of Vesuvius in 79 A. D., modern excavators have found charred book rolls. An experience of Paul's in Ephesus shows that popular literature was not neglected. A number of sorcerers carried on their business in that city, offering their hocus-pocus to a credulous people in return for money. They were consulted during sickness, or to restore lost property, to injure a hated enemy, or to prosper business, and they performed all kinds of things, possible and impossible. They had books of charms, that is, collections of all kinds of mysterious prescriptions, powerful exorcisms, and terrible curses. Paul opposed these mysterious gentlemen and made such a good impression that many of them were converted. The result was that they brought out their books, piled them up in a public place, and burned them. According to Acts 19:19 these books were valued at fifteen hundred pounds sterling. We can gather from this narrative how bulky was this magic literature, how widely it was circulated and read among the people.

In the home of Christianity in the stricter sense, in Palestine, a great deal was written and read at this time. Disregarding the works of the Jewish authors and the writing done in public and private life, we must lay special emphasis on the fact that in Palestine a certain book, a distinct "scripture," enjoyed unique reverence and formed the central point of the whole religious life. Among the Jews in Palestine we find a "Holy Book," a "Holy Scripture," taken over from the Fathers, or, more precisely, a collection of the Holy Scriptures of the past in the Hebrew language. They were the same scriptures as those which we usually call the "Old" Testament. Preëminent among the books of the Old Testament were the first; as the "Law" they were the highest authorities for every believing son of Israel. The voice of the living God Himself could be heard in every letter of the Law; every point and line was honored and respected as the expression of the divine will. The words of the prophets and the other holy scriptures had also a unique authority, and, like the law, they were read in the divine services on the Sabbaths. With the Law they formed the basis of the religious lessons in the Temple and in the synagogues. A special class devoted itself to the study and exposition of the Holy Scriptures, that is, the professional scribes. The guidance of the people was entirely in their hands; they possessed, not only the truth of the Law, Prophets, and Writings, but, in addition, an oral tradition which added much to the written one.

Also the Man from whom the greatest spiritual impulse has come, an impulse which is felt through two thousand years of Christian history, Jesus of Nazareth, in common with His disciples, had the greatest reverence for the Holy Scriptures. It is not insignificant, in this connection, that in the narrative of Luke we find Him when He was twelve years old, in the Temple sitting among the learned, listening to them and asking questions. We gather from the words of Jesus, which have been handed down to us, that He was intimately acquainted with the contents of the Holy Scriptures, and had the greatest love for them. Yet He did not bow down to the letter of the Law, for example, the Sabbath commandment; He performed works of relief and love to His neighbor on the Sabbath. But still he would not annul the Holy Scriptures. He even confessed once, "Think not that I came to destroy the law or the prophets: I came not to destroy, but to fulfill. For verily I say unto you, Till heaven and earth pass away, one jot or one tittle shall in no wise pass away from the law" (Matt. 5:17 ff.).

Let us look back for a moment: Christianity arose at a time when a great deal was being written, in an age of extensive literature and of vast public and private writing. Christianity originated in a country in which a book, as Holy Scriptures, enjoyed unique reverence because men heard the voice of God Himself in its lines. Jesus of Nazareth, the Prophet of the Gospel, and His circle of disciples paid all respect and reverence to this Holy Book, as their inheritance from their fathers and forefathers. All this is certain.

THE ORIGIN

But it is also quite as certain that the Gospel itself did not begin with a sacred book, not even with a single written page, or one inscription on a stone or in bronze.

* * *

Jesus Himself has not left a single line written by his own hand, and He never commanded one of his intimate friends, saying, "Take a pen and write down the words which I say unto thee." Only once, in the narratives, do we hear of Him writing, and that when He was called to pronounce a sentence on an adulteress. But even then, He did not write on papyrus, or parchment, or clay, or marble, but in the dust (John 8:6–8). In a few moments children, a puff of wind, or the feet of a hurrying traveler had blotted out the written words of Jesus forever.

Of course Jesus took up the pen occasionally. As a child he learned the Aleph, Beth, and Gimel; later, as a man, He now and again signed a document and possibly He wrote a letter. But if Jesus wrote He certainly wrote no book, still less a sacred book for future generations. Jesus is not a man of literature, and in that respect He differs from many of His famous contemporaries. Neither is Jesus the author of a sacred book. In this respect He differs from other prophets, and from many of the great founders of religions. It is part of the unsurpassable greatness of the historical Jesus that He did not come forward as a lawgiver with sections and paragraphs, but rather as a sower who scattered with blessing hands the divine seed over the field. This seed He left to itself, so convinced was He of its vitality (Mark 4:26 ff.). The Jesus who wrote no book but staked all on the Spirit and the living Word surpassed all the book prophets. If Christianity began with Jesus, then it can be said that it did not begin with a book. Christianity is older than the sacred book of Christianity, Christianity is older than the New Testament. In the beginning was, not the book and not the letter; in the beginning was the Word and the Spirit. First of all

THE ORIGIN

Christianity learned to pray, afterward it learned to write—just like the children. The prayer, "Our Father," is older than the New Testament; the Gospel is older than the Gospels. Thus we place a non-literary, a pre-literary period in the history of Primitive Christianity, before the literary period in which the first Christian books were written.

The classic period of Early Christianity is the pre-literary period. Classical Early Christianity is first of all a non-literary, spiritual movement, in contrast to the literary culture of the world around it. Theological scholars have brought it far too much into contact with this literary culture. We must emphasize the contrast, and in this direction lies the task of scientific research of the future, and here also is the seed of a fruitful, practical appreciation of Early Christianity.

From this it can be said that Christianity, in its origin, is not a book-religion, as many have asserted. Later there came a period in which it became a book-religion. But originally, it was not so. The Book, the New Testament, is really the result of Christianity. It is true that Jesus and His followers honored a book, the old Bible of the people of Israel, as a divine authority. But the fact that it owned the Old Testament does not distinguish Early Christianity from Judaism. What distinguished Early Christianity from Judaism was, not the possession of a book, but rather the possession of the personality of Jesus of Nazareth. With Jesus everything depends on the vitality of the Word, on deep thinking, on a living, winged Spirit, on the simple, triumphant Truth. In the beginning was, not the book, in the beginning was the Word which had become flesh in Jesus of Nazareth.

※ ※ ※

Again, the second great figure which stands clearly outlined on the threshold of Christianity, Paul of Tarsus, "the Apostle of Jesus Christ," also belongs to the non-literary, pre-literary period of Christianity. Paul is not a man of literature, although he

THE ORIGIN

has been treated as such by many scholars.

That he has been so considered is, perhaps, pardonable. We possess quite a number of letters from the Apostle, and these have come down to us as part of a book. And then, unfortunately without making clear the great distinction between what is literary and what is not, these letters were designated as epistolary literature, and Paul as the greatest author of Early Christianity. But both designations are momentous misjudgments.

Between the genuine, confidential letter, only one copy of which is sent to the addressee, and the literary epistle, re-duplicated into hundreds of copies, and intended to interest the public, there is the same difference as between life and art. The genuine letter is a reflection of life, just like a confidential conversation between two friends. The literary epistle is a piece of art, like a Platonic dialogue.

The letters of Paul have often been treated as literary epistles, but really they are not such. Paul's letters are genuine, confidential letters, not intended for the public or for posterity. They were not even intended for the Christian public of that time. They were for the addressees only. When Paul wishes a certain letter to be read in another community he expressly says so (Col. 4:16), and the non-literary character of his letter does not suffer in any way.

The letters of Paul were real non-literary letters. Innumerable mistakes made in the study of Paul arise from the fact that his writings have been treated as literary. Too often they have been regarded as dogmatic pamphlets, as theological declarations each one supplementing the other to form a great, complete system. And because they contain, like all letters, parts which are irreconcilable with each other, they have been declared, partly or nearly all, to be "not genuine."

The closer relation of modern study to real life, and a better knowledge of the working and the possibilities of a great man's mind, has led to the abandonment of the doctrinaire mis-

THE ORIGIN

conceptions of an older research which was out of touch with the world. The essential genuineness of Paul's letters will be admitted when the irreconcilable parts in them are seen as proofs of their originality.

Real difficulties remain only in the case of the so-called Pastoral letters, those to Timothy and Titus. I can only just touch the problem here, for time will not allow of a detailed treatment. But it seems to me certain that also in the Pastoral letters we have, at least, a good number of genuine lines by Paul.

The origin of the individual letters of Paul also forms a very rich chapter of Bible study, which I can only glance at hastily. I would answer the main problems of this chapter something like this:

The majority of the letters of Paul which we have were written during the last decade of his life, under the Roman Emperors Claudius and Nero. The chronology of the individual letters is not yet fully ascertained. Positive dates are given in most modern books, but they are only of a more or less hypothetical nature. Through the discovery of an inscription in Delphi we are, however, in a position to make the chronology of Paul and of Early Christianity more certain. I have published the inscription in facsimile and dealt with it in detail in my book *Paul*. It enables us to ascertain the date of office of the proconsul who is called Gallio in chapter eighteen of Acts, and from that the date of Paul's first sojourn in Corinth, that is, from the beginning of the year fifty A. D. until the end of the summer in the year fifty-one A. D.

The two earliest of Paul's letters which we possess were written at this time—the First and Second Thessalonians.

With regard to the remaining letters of Paul I have not yet come to a definite conclusion in my studies. But I believe, if the real chronology is to be ascertained, that there are quite a number of questions to be raised besides the usual ones. In particular an imprisonment or divers imprisonments of Paul in Ephesus should be taken into consideration, during which the so-called imprisonment letters were written, namely, the letters to Philemon and to the Colossians, the so-called letter to the Ephesians (which is really a letter to the church at Laodicea) and the letter to the Philippians. Most scholars place these letters in the time of Paul's imprisonment in Rome; but I believe that this view is now untenable; they belong to Ephesus between the time of the composition of the first and the second letters to the Corinthians.

I would offer the following as the historical order of the letters of Paul, omitting the Pastoral letters:

I and II Thessalonians written in Corinth 50–51 A. D.

I Corinthians
Galatians
Philemon
Colossians
So-called Ephesians (Laodicea)
Philippians

} All these six letters probably written in Ephesus between 52 and 55 A. D.

II Corinthians written in Macedonia in summer 55 A. D.

Romans, Chapters 1–15, written in Corinth in winter 55–56 A. D.

Romans, Chapter 16 (which is, in my opinion, a separate letter to Ephesus), written in Corinth in winter 55–56 A. D.

These dates should not be taken as final.

With regard to the external circumstances of the origin of Paul's letters it can be said that they were written without much preparation or anxious reflection, and without a carefully worked-out plan or a conscious striving after rhetorical effect. He dictated the majority of them to a scribe, perhaps a few of them while working at his trade as a tent maker. Then he would insert a few lines in his large, clumsy, laborer's handwriting—compare Galatians 6:11: "See what big letters I make, when I write you in my own hand" (Moffatt's translation). Some letters were written in great haste, possibly during a journey, for example, II Corinthians, which is much more vivid because of that than the letter to the Romans, which Paul probably wrote in a period of peace and quiet. He can hardly have made it a rule to duplicate his letters for others. Only one copy of the letter would be written, and that one would be sent to the addressee. In a few cases he may have retained a draft of the letter.

The more we recognize the natural, spontaneous, and unliterary origin of the letters of Paul, the better prepared we are to understand them. They originated in exactly the same way as every other real letter does, or at least, should; not through a desire for great literary publicity, but through the necessity for personal communication between man and man. Like every other genuine letter, when it is free from affectation, and is naïve in the good sense of the word, it reproduces the personality of the writer, sometimes faintly, other times clearly. Such are the letters of Paul. Every one of them is a picture of him, not a small volume from the collected works of Paul the author, but an item from the life of the greatest of Christian missionaries.

The later fortunes of the letters of Paul are the same as those of letters in general. Part of them were lost, the remainder were in the hands of the addressees in Corinth, Philippi, or Rome, or Paul himself had a draft of a few of them. But as the figure of the Apostle, after his death, came to fill an increasingly important place in the thoughts and reverence of his followers, greater importance was attached to the remainder of his letters. Probably before the end of the first century, those Pauline letters which could be found were collected and published, and so it became possible at a later time to insert them in the canon of a Sacred Book. But this collecting and publishing did not change the real character of the letters of Paul in any sense; they remained genuine letters, whether they were in the possession of the small churches in Corinth and Galatia, or, a century later, were well known to the whole of Christendom as part of the New Testament which was gradually being formed. Paul is a letter writer and not a man of letters; with Jesus he belongs to the non-literary period of Christianity.

* * *

It seems time for us to speak at last of the New Testament, or of a Christian book or books. We set out to describe the origin of the book, but, so far, we have only said that Jesus and Paul wrote no books. But there is a very good reason for my dwelling so long with the non-literary period of Primitive Christianity. I feel that the majority of scholars have said far too little about the non-literary period of Christianity. Setting out with the opinion that everything that is written is literature, they have often badly misrepresented it, and especially the figure of Paul. Therefore, it will be for our good to put that side in the background for once, and determine to picture the origin of the New Testament so that we see at the beginning, not the era of books, but the era of the book-less creative personalities; the period, not of the letter, but of the Spirit of God working in the living words of the Master, of the Spirit of Christ working in the words of His Apostle.

So we can distinguish three periods in the history of the origin of the New Testament:

1. The pre-literary period of the Gospel of Jesus and of His Apostle, Paul.
2. The literary period of the Gospels and other Apostolic books.
3. The period of the formation of the Canon, which brought together the non-literary and the literary remains of the Apostolic period into the Canon of the New Testament.

We have yet to sketch roughly the main lines of the last two periods.

II

THE ORIGIN OF THE NEW TESTAMENT (B)

II

THE ORIGIN OF THE NEW TESTAMENT (B)

THE beginnings of the literary period lie in obscurity. But this much can be said with certainty, that no fixed, mechanical line can be drawn between the non-literary and the literary periods. The literary period began already in the lifetime of the Apostle Paul. He himself was non-literary, but we see the beginnings of Christian literature in the first Apostolic generation. I use the word "literature" here in the sense of writings composed for the public in definite, fixed "forms." What has come down to us of the early Christian literature enables us to recognize three characteristic features which I believe to be of great importance to our whole scientific attitude to the New Testament:

Firstly: the old Christian literature is not world-literature, but literature for Christians.

Secondly: although it is Christian literature, it is not canonical literature for the completion of the Old Testament.

Finally: corresponding to the social structure of Early Christianity it is primarily popular literature and not art literature for the educated. This last fact is of the greatest importance.

Of the literary "forms" used by the first Christian authors, one, the Gospel book, is a Christian innovation. Others are taken over from Jewish literature—the Sacred Chronicle and the Book of Revelation. Others were taken from the world-literature (perhaps through Jewish literature)—the Epistle and the Religious Tract.

* * *

The records of Jesus formed the first beginnings of Christian literature, as, for example, the Aramaic collection of the sayings of Jesus by the Apostle Matthew, which has not been handed down to us. For us, the three Gospels of Matthew, Mark, and Luke (the Synoptic Gospels) stand first. They bear the unmistakable characteristics of simple, popular books in which the contents and not the form is significant. And that is the secret of their influence on all periods. They cannot be treated as critical, historical books in the modern sense. They are primarily story books, obviously the result of bringing together unchecked the different parts of the tradition about Jesus which were circulated among the people, at first orally, and later in a fixed written form.

The Gospel of Mark seems to be the earliest, written about the year 70 A. D. by Mark, companion of the Apostle Peter. It was used by the other two Evangelists who may have written during the last thirty years of the First Century. Probably the Gospel of Matthew also used the collection of the words of Jesus by Matthew. Beside the early Gospels, Luke had at his disposal other excellent sources which were most used by Mark and Matthew. The other book written by Luke, the Acts of the Apostles, is also a popular book. It must have been written at some period before the letters of Paul had been collected and published. But the narrator had other good sources, especially his own diary of his travels, which is employed in the "we" narratives. The Acts of the Apostles is the first history of Christian missions. That it was written, like the Gospel which bears his name, by Luke the Physician, the companion of Paul, seems to me highly probable.

In contrast to the Synoptic Gospels stands the Gospel of John. The Gospels of Matthew, Mark, and Luke could be called the workday Gospels. The Gospel of John is the Sunday Gospel. Here we can hear the festival bells ringing, now softer and again louder. The historian has to consider it in connection with three other texts which bear the name of John, those which are usually called the Johannine letters. Not one of the four texts contains the name of John, it is only found in the titles, which do not belong to the original text but are added by the compilers of the Canon. But in the second and third letter of John the writer calls himself "Presbyteros," that is, either "the old man," or in the technical sense, "the elder." That this man is the author also of the first letter and the Gospel is shown, not only by the style which is so unmistakably original that it may serve for once as the criterion of the critic, but also by the religious contents of the four texts, which is throughout of the same cast. The important task of the study of John is to grasp this religious character of the Johannine writings.

And in this connection it may be said: the Johannine picture of Christ distinguishes itself in a very marked way from that of the Synoptic Gospels. In the first place the outline of the life of Jesus is quite different, and, besides, almost all the transmitted sayings of Jesus are different from those of the Synoptic writers, while on the other hand their general character agrees to an extraordinary degree with the words of John in the first letter.

In the first three Gospels there stands before us a figure of flesh and blood, in the Gospel of John an ethereal, spiritual figure. We know the figure. It is the Christ which Paul had also seen, Christ the Lord, Christ the Spirit. And so the Gospel of John is in a real sense the Pauline Gospel, the great reflection of the Christ religion of Paul. Certainly it is not the growing, still surging Christianity of the Pauline letters, but a complete, clarified, calm Christianity. Yet it is Pauline Christianity through and through even to a startling agreement with the favorite expressions of Paul. Therefore it is later than Paul. In the Gospel of John the non-literary Pauline Christianity has become literary. Literary, but not philosophical (in spite of the Logos) or artificial. Even the Gospel of John is a popular book, as is shown especially by its language, and just because of that it has had great influence on the churches of all centuries. Here again it is necessary to combat the traditional errors of research: it is essential to recognize the Gospel of John again in all its simplicity. In that way the polemic and apologetic designs of the author become obvious.

He is struggling against different menacing groups: the disciples of John the Baptist, the Gnostics, the Jews of the big synagogues of Asia Minor, and the lukewarm, half-hearted members of the Church. After all, in the background of his message the beginnings of an antagonism between John and Peter, that is, between Ephesus and Rome, between the East and the West, become perceptible if you observe what John says about Peter and which traditions about Peter he omits. Behind many of his negative sentences you can see the opposition against which he fights the good fight of faith.

Besides this it was the author's intention to provide for a lectionary, somewhat like an "evangeliarium," for the divine service. You will do justice to him if you regard his book as a series of pericopes, of stories, often unconnected with another, not as a connected history.

In the same way the first "letter" of John, that great confession of the love of God and of fellow man, which is quite in the same spirit as the Gospel of John, is not without such designs. This very informal text is not a letter, neither is it a literary epistle, but a simple religious tract.

The other two texts, the second and third letters of John, are genuine letters, and as such they are valuable witnesses to the personality of the "Presbyteros" whom we have to thank for all the Johannine writings.

Who, then, is this great stranger? Is he the Apostle John, or John the Presbyteros, or another John, or is he a Christian who writes under the cover of an Apostolic name? I will not venture to answer this question of authorship with unconditional certainty. But it seems to me very probable that the author was a personal disciple of Jesus, perhaps John the Presbyteros. This John was the outstanding leader of the Church of Asia in the last years of the First Century. He was not the sentimental, tearful old man of the traditional representation, but one of God's champions of heroic intolerance and at the same time the deepest Christ-mystic.

The book which now stands at the end of the New Testament, the Revelation of John, is, in every sense, a book of the people. Its literary form was already popular in every sphere influenced by the Jews or Jewish Christians. It is clear from the book itself that the author was a Christian from Asia Minor. Probably he had become a Christian through Judaism. In any case he was a prophet of a unique, living piety. I do not think it impossible that this book is also the work of John the Presbyteros. He wrote his book during a period of persecution and dispersion in the last decade of the First Century. It is not improbable that he incorporated in his book older visions of the period before the year 70 A. D. The author wrote under the conviction that the Exalted Master was behind him, and that he himself was called to communicate the Will of the Master to the churches.

* * *

Further documents belonging to the end of the First Century and the beginning of the Second, which reflect the same power of Christ, are the other literary remains of Early Christianity--the two Epistles of Peter, that of Jude and of James, and the so-called Epistle to the Hebrews. Here we have to deal not with real unliterary letters, as in the case of the Pauline letters, but with literary epistles and pamphlets written for Christendom, forcible words of warning and of comfort. Yet we have in the Epistle of James a document of a decidedly popular nature. The question as to the authorship and origin of these books, which all seem to be strongly influenced by the meanwhile published collection of the Pauline letters, is much disputed. I believe that the Epistles of Peter, of Jude, and of James are pamphlets which were written at the end of the First or the beginning of the Second Century under the cover of the names of the early Apostles. They are not "pseudonymous" in the bad sense of the word. They are "heteronymous" according to a well-known literary practice of Antiquity.

* * *

The so-called "Epistle to the Hebrews" is not an epistle but a religious tract. Its author is not known by name, but, owing to his theological training, he forms such a striking figure in the series of early Christian authors that we can say that his little book had a unique significance in the history of Early Christianity. It is, on account of its polished form and scholarly contents, the first example of what we can consider Christian art-literature. That means that, with this book, Christianity took the first step out of the class in which it had its roots.

The roots of Christianity lay in the lower and middle classes; Jesus was a carpenter and Paul was a tent maker. It was the simple people of Galilee who surrounded Jesus, and the churches of Paul were made up of slaves, of laborers, and the unknown poor of the big cities. Well-to-do and well-educated Christians were exceptions in the early times. This social structure of Early Christianity is reflected clearly in its literature; the language, the literary types, and the contents are popular.

With the little book to the Hebrews, which was followed by others of a similar nature in the Second Century, Early Christianity stepped out of this class. A development of great historical importance began: Christianity began to take up ancient philosophy and education.

* * *

So we have reached the point which gives us a glimpse of the last epoch of the history of the origin of the New Testament. The Christianity which had taken up education is the

THE ORIGIN

Christianity organized in the world for the fight against the world powers, the Christianity which was, in the narrow and full sense of the word, ecclesiastical. It is no longer the community of the saints of the old Pauline churches, who waited with ardent longing for the end of the world and the early return of the Master. It is rather a lawfully organized corporation, with many officials and institutions, which prepared itself for a long future in this world.

This ecclesiastical Christianity, this corporation church, which from the beginning of the Second Century onward distinguished itself more and more from the simple Apostolic corpus church, began immediately to collect the remains of the writings of the early period. It brought them together gradually, on the model of the Old Testament, into a Sacred Book, into the Canon of the New Testament.

We have distinguished three periods in the history of the origin of the New Testament: the non-literary period, the literary period, and the period of the formation of the Canon. The first two periods produced the texts, non-literary and literary. The third period brought these texts together into the New Testament taking its place side by side with the Old Testament.

* * *

The Pauline letters and the Gospels and the other early Christian books were never composed with a view of forming a New Testament at some future time. Neither Jesus nor Paul left behind a New Bible, to take the place of the Old, or to take its place beside it. Both remained true to the Old Testament, and Jesus during His early life was the authority of His disciples for everything else. The fact that Jesus Himself and His disciples held fast to the authority of the Old Testament Canon does not contradict our statement that the earliest Christian period was a pre-canonical period. That the earliest Christians stood reverently on the ground of the Old Testament is no characteristic feature by which early Christianity distinguished itself from Judaism. On the contrary, the reverence shown to the Old Testament is a clear indication of the close historical connection between Christianity and Judaism. What is new, what is characteristic, and what is of unique significance for the future in Early Christianity is not as we saw before, the Jewish Bible, but the personality and the Gospel of Jesus of Nazareth.

The Glorified Jesus remained the infallible authority for His followers. We know that especially through the indications given by Paul in his letters. It is true that Paul stood, like every pious Jewish Christian, firmly on the ground of the Old Testament, even in every polemic against the Law. But his highest authority is the living Jesus Christ, exalted to the Lordship of the Spirit. From Him Paul had received his revelations, and from Him, he knew, the believers received the life force. For He is the body and His followers are the members. Paul, and with him the earliest

Christians, did not refer to a written tradition of a Jesus of the past. They were able to receive "grace for grace" from the fullness of the present living Christ. Paul was in touch with a higher world, with the Redeemer who had become Spirit, and in Him with the Living God.

Nevertheless Paul was not without a highly honored tradition of the words and deeds of the earthly Jesus. Where a saying of Jesus was available to the Apostle, whether it was from oral or written tradition, it removed all doubts for him. He always set the words of Jesus tower-high above his own opinion. In these traditions of the words and deeds of Jesus, which circulated among the Christians, at first orally and later in writing, lay the first forebodings of a future Christian Canon. The first accounts of the sayings of Jesus certainly were not composed with the intention of supplementing the Old Testament with a New, but rather out of reverence to Jesus. It was a necessity of the Christ cult to safeguard all information concerning Him. As, in time, those who had seen and heard Jesus became fewer the more valuable became the written tradition. When the rushing torrent of the wonderful revelations and the living force of the *epigoni* began to spend itself, the more indispensable became the quiet and clear stream which rippled in the words of the Saviour.

One thing in particular must have strengthened the impulse to canonize the words of Jesus. That is the conviction that the Second Coming of the Lord was not in the near future. Paul and the believers of his time expected the day in which they would see the returning Lord face to face, in the near future. As the hope of later generations moderated, they looked more away from the returning Lord, whom they would probably never see personally, to Him who had come, whose voice they could hear in the pages of the Gospels. They prepared for a long future for which it was necessary to have a sound tradition of what He had commanded and accomplished. And it is easy to understand that later in a poorer and quieter period the remains of the writings of an Apostle or of any other man of the Apostolic time became very valuable. For example, what remained here and there in the churches of the letters of Paul would then be collected. The churches transmitted the valuable sheets which they possessed from the hand of the holy man to other churches. Thus the confidential lines of Paul became well known throughout Christendom. Still Luke did not know of a collection of Pauline letters. Perhaps we are allowed to link the name of Timothy with the making of the oldest collection. Probably it was published after the Acts of the Apostles. And now it had great influence on the Catholic Epistles, the Johannine writings, and the Apostolic Fathers.

* * *

The Gospels and the Apostolic writings were then the two groups which came to be regarded more and more as the authority in the post-Apostolic age. And these two groups were the crystallizing point in the making of the New Testament. We do not know when the crystallizing began, but we shall not be far wrong when we say in the first decade of the Second Century A. D. Neither do we know where the first collection of the writings of the Apostolic age was made, nor what writings were included in that collection. It will hardly be maintained that there was a uniform procedure in this connection. As in later centuries, so at this time of the formation of a Christian Canon, men would have different opinions as to the canonical dignity of the different books.

If one would examine very carefully the sources one would find that already in the earliest times of the formation of the Canon there were serious differences concerning the order and dignity of certain books between the East and the West, between the Churches of Ephesus and of Rome, and generally Rome became victor in this controversy, her victory being symbolized by the facts that Paul's letter to the Romans now stands in the beginning of the Pauline Canon and that in many codices some other Pauline letters received the incorrect but effective certificate of origin: "written from Rome."

It is certain that the first motives for forming a Christian Canon were of a more religious nature. It was an obvious necessity of the adoring love for Jesus and His Apostles that what could be saved of their words should be saved before those irrecoverable words were lost in oblivion.

But the interests of the Christ-cult became more and more dominant. When the time of the first gifts of grace, the first fire, the first love was past, as the organized church entered into the fight with the world and false teaching, then as an organization it required fixed rules and standards. A Canon of its own was essential to the Church. The collection of the legacies of Jesus and the Apostolic time, which was started by the piety of the believers, was carried on with great zeal by the men of the Church which was becoming more and more rigidly organized. It was the needs of the Church which hastened the process of canonizing the early Christian writings. The genesis of the New Testament runs parallel with the genesis of the old Christian Catholic Church. The separate parts of the Canon were the work of the pre-ecclesiastical, Apostolic Christianity; the Canon itself was the work of ecclesiastical Christianity. This development is the same as the origin of Christian dogma. Christianity did not come into the world as dogma; dogma is the product of a long period of Christian development which ran parallel with the development of the Church. Church, Canon, and Dogma, these Three, belong together historically.

* * *

We can indicate more precisely those parts of the Canon which were admitted generally in the earliest times. They were, on one hand, the Gospels of Matthew, Mark, Luke, and John; the Acts of the Apostles and the letters of Paul on the other hand. These two groups were the fixed backbone of the New Testament in the middle of the Second Century, and there was no hesitation at any time concerning them. But the other writings had to struggle more or less for their places in the Canon. We possess a list of canonical scriptures of the last half of the Second Century. It contains the four Gospels, the Acts of the Apostles, thirteen letters of Paul, the Epistle of Jude, the first and second letters of John, the Wisdom of Solomon (strangely), the Revelation of John, the Revelation of Peter (this last not recognized by all of "Us"), and similarly the Shepherd of Hermas. The Epistle to the Hebrews, the first and second Epistles of Peter, the third letter of John, and the Epistle of James are not mentioned. I confine myself to this one example. Here we see a number of writings which we do not have

THE ORIGIN 63

in our New Testament, and a number of writings are included in our New Testament which had not been included at that time.

* * *

Two books were the subjects of great controversy in the Early Church: the Revelation of John and the Epistle to the Hebrews. The Revelation of John was attacked especially by the Greek Christians; the most distinguished church scholars raised their voices against admitting it into the Canon. On the other hand the Latin Christians took the same attitude toward the Epistle to the Hebrews, and regarded it with grave suspicion. Also the other Catholic Epistles were partly rejected and partly admitted; at any rate, a long time passed before they succeeded in obtaining a fixed place in the Canon.

In the third district of the Church, in Syria, we find other peculiarities. There even the four Gospels went into the background behind a Harmony of the Gospels, the Diatessaron of Tatian, and the letters of Paul were extended by the addition of a correspondence with the Corinthians which is not genuine.

* * *

Thus it is possible to observe a distinct inclination toward forming a New Testament Canon in the first centuries of the Christian Church. We can also see a few points of direction toward which this development moved. But it is quite as clear that there was great uncertainty with regard to the question which of the scriptures really belonged to the New Testament.

When did this uncertainty cease? Strictly it never ceased in the Early Church. To speak of "the" settlement of the Canon in the Early Church is misleading. In spite of all the measures used officially, in practice the uncertainty as to the limits of the New Testament remained, to a great extent in Eastern Christendom, and to a less extent in Latin Christendom. In Latin Christendom it was three synods of the Fourth and Fifth centuries which determined the number and order of the Books of the New Testament as we have them today: the synod of Hippo in the year 393 A. D., and the synods of Carthage in 397 A. D. and 419 A. D. Still, in the Middle Ages, in many manuscripts of the Vulgate, that is, of the official Latin Bible, there was to be found a spurious letter of Paul, the letter to the Laodiceans.

* * *

It was the period of the Reformation which gave to the Roman Catholic Church a conclusive Canon. After the old opinions and doubts had partly reappeared the Tridentine Council in 1546 declared the entire contents of the Vulgate, without distinction, to be divine; in the New Testament twenty-seven books: four Gospels, the Acts of the Apostles, fourteen letters of Paul, seven Catholic Epistles, and the Revelation of John.

Among the Reformers we find a vigorous criticism of the traditional Canon. Luther with the native courage of his faith made an excellent criticism, especially in his preface to the German New Testament in 1522. He substantiated a difference of value in the books and created a positive criterion for judging the Canon. He asked which books "revealed Christ." Zwingli and Calvin also criticized the Canon. Martin Chemnitz, 1586, grouped seven New Testament Antilegomena, that is, books whose canonical value is doubtful. Similarly others in the Seventeenth Century spoke of "deutero-canonical" books of the New Testament, that is, canonical books of the second grade.

Also the English translator Tyndale adopted Luther's criticism of some of the books of the New Testament. But the consolidation of the Canon of the English Bible was later facilitated by the declaration of the Thirty-nine Articles of 1562 that all the books of the New Testament "*ut vulgo recepti sunt*" are canonical, thus confirming the received Catholic New Testament Canon.

Since about 1700 the New Testament in its

Catholic form has also been naturalized by the Protestant Christians of Germany and that without any official measures. How this has come about is not yet explained in detail. The forming of the doctrine of inspiration and also the enormous circulation of printed Bibles have had great influence in this fixing of the Canon. If handwriting had a subjective nature, printing had an objective and standardizing nature.

It is only with regard to the order of the books of the New Testament, which is not yet uniform among the churches, that we find the influence of old difficulties still remaining.

* * *

If you take a German New Testament in your hand and find out, for example, what place the Epistle to the Hebrews occupies in it, and if you compare it then with two or three other German or English editions of the New Testament, you will perhaps see that it occupies a different place in them. And that insignificant detail will perhaps remind you of a noble history of nearly two thousand years. Like the lapping of the last wave on the sea after a long storm, so is this minor uncertainty as to the order of the books in our printed New Testaments.

Once again the thoughtful reader of the New Testament thinks of the main stages of that great history; of the days when the Gospel and early Christianity had nothing to do with books. Then of the period when the popular books of the Evangelists and of the other Apostolic writers were written for the uneducated, simple people of the Christian brotherhood; and of the time when a well-educated Christian brought out in the Epistle to the Hebrews, for the first time, a work of Christian art-literature. Finally, we think of the decades and centuries which gradually formed the Canon of the New Testament from the remains of the great past and which, by rescuing the earliest documents of our religion for mankind, accomplished what has only one parallel in the history of the Early Church: the cloud of martyrs who consented to die for their faith.

* * *

This backward glance at the history of the origin of the New Testament is extraordinarily instructive for every man who is deeply interested in higher things. The history of the origin of the New Testament reflects again the powerful historical process which we call the history of Christianity. Clearly we see in the development of the New Testament the development of our religion: from the Gospel preached to the fishermen and publicans on the shores of the Lake of Genesareth, to the organized Church of the Church Fathers and Councils. This process was one of cooling and stiffening. Spirit very often became letter, prayer became a liturgy, gifts of love became tithes. The Reformation, which again across the centuries grasped the New Testament, grasped at a book which when studied externally and superficially looks like a law book, but which when understood internally and deeply investigated presents to us again personalities in whom the revelation of the classical antiquity is embodied. The Reformation made the hard metal again into a glowing stream. Through the Book it prevented Christianity from remaining what it has often become in the world, a religion of a book, a religion of the letter.

And that will always be the effect of our Holy Book, when it is approached in the same spirit. The contents of this Book deny its book-character. Through the letter it gives us a glimpse of a unique personal life whose support and inspiration are in the living God.

III

THE LANGUAGE OF THE NEW TESTAMENT

III

THE LANGUAGE OF THE NEW TESTAMENT

IN THE first lectures on the origins of the New Testament the characteristic standpoint of my conception was that the New Testament did not originate in the sphere of ancient literary culture. It is rather the reflection of that which flowed out of the souls of non-literary, simple prophets of the people in a period of unparalleled religious awakening.

This standpoint is in strong contrast to the usual method of treatment in former times. Because the New Testament appeared as a book, and a book written in Greek, it was put side by side with the other old Greek books as a matter of course. When thus raised to the sphere of ancient art literature, the New Testament gained a notably unique position, quite an exceptional position with regard to language. When I speak now on the subject of the language of the New Testament, I do not deal with a remote philological problem for philological experts. The problem is important enough to be of interest to every theologian and to the educated man who is not a theologian. For a great part of the essence of the New Testament lies hidden in its language. Whoever has understood the nature of the language of the New Testament has also understood a great deal of the essence of the New Testament and of Early Christianity.

* * *

With what does this problem of the language of the New Testament deal?

The old methods, which placed the New Testament among the literary works of the ancient world, gave to the language of the New Testament a peculiar, exceptional place. And this seemed to be quite justified, because there really was a very strong contrast between it and the language of the literature belonging to the period in which the New Testament originated.

In the literature of the Imperial period the predominant tendency was the so-called "Atticism," a cultural phenomenon which has lasted through the centuries down to the present time, and to-day its influence can be seen, for example, in the unfortunate language controversies in Greece, and also in the methods of some of our higher schools.

Atticism originated with the idea that the classical Attic literature was the highest point in Greek culture, and that the standard for the modeling of the Greek language is to be found in it. Therefore Atticism was anxious to write a modeled Greek, which for the most part was an imitation of the classical Attic. While the colloquial language had become very different from the stilted art language of the Attic classic (and indeed the colloquial language was quite different in the classical period itself), the Atticists of the early Imperial period wrote the artificial book language of imitated Attic.

On the other hand there are very few Atticisms in the New Testament. In the majority of its books there is no trace of conscious Attic refining. Instead we find much of the bluntness and license of the colloquial wild-growing Greek. But this general character of the language of the New Testament has been misjudged. The obvious difference between it and the Greek of the Atticists has been explained in two ways, either by saying that it is "tired" Greek and "bad" Greek, or by isolating it as "Jewish" Greek or "Biblical" Greek or "New Testament" Greek. This was done not only by theologians but also by philologists. I remember the famous Greek scholar, Dr. Friedrich Blass of the University of Halle, who, even as late as 1894, declared that "the New Testament Greek should be recognized as something distinct and subject to its own laws."

Both these theories, that of the "tired"

Greek and that of the "Jewish" Greek, have proved to be fetters in the study, and particularly in the exegesis of the New Testament, where in endless cases the special exegetical questions have been wrongly answered because of this isolation.

That these fetters have been removed, and that to-day the international study of the Bible, both in theology and in philology, has reached the correct point of view, is the result of the study of those important new discoveries of non-literary written memorials belonging to the time of the New Testament which I mentioned before: the texts on stones, on papyri, on ostraca, and in other forms. Greek inscriptions had been known long before, and some scholars had already begun to use them for the elucidation of the New Testament. But the inscriptions are often modeled according to the traditions of the literary language and the offices of the authorities. Now, as a rule, the language of the papyri and the ostraca is the unstilted language of the people.

And these texts have yet an additional value in that they can be dated, in the majority of cases, to the year, and often to the day. But it would be quite incorrect to surmise that these texts were written in a specifically Egyptian Greek. Of course peculiarities of the Egyptian Greek existed, but in general the language of the papyri is the Greek *Koine* of the Mediterranean world.

The proof for this statement lies in the fact that the Greek of these Egyptian papyri and ostraca on the one hand, and the Greek of Syria, Asia Minor, and Southern Europe on the other hand, have been found to agree in innumerable points. They were days full of joy for the discoverer, full of new insights, when, on the theological side, these parallels were first established and their significance was first seen. I may here refer to the great coöperation of Continental and English-speaking investigators, and for the details I may refer you to my books *Bible Studies* and *Light from the Ancient East,* as well as the excellent works of Dr. James Hope Moulton, Dr. George Milligan, Dr. A. T. Robertson, and many others.

The result of these investigations, in which, of course, numbers of scholars from other countries have taken part, is chiefly this: that in the New Testament we have to deal, not with "tired" Greek, nor "Jewish" Greek, but rather with the wild-growing speech of the people at the different stages of its development. It has been shown that it was a great mistake to take for granted that the Greek language reached its highest point in the classical Attic, and that afterward there was only deterioration. The case is really this: that when Greek came to be used in literature there were two chief forms of it, one which always existed among the masses of the people, the living speech of the people which always spread further, and above it, the literary language modeled according to artificial rules.

We have no documents, or at least only very few, in the people's language of the old period, because it never found expression in literature. But it is obvious that the sailors of Athens, or the merchants of the Ionian colonies, or the peasants of the Peloponnesus never spoke the language as it was written by Demosthenes or Thucydides. In the papyri and the ostraca on the one hand, and in the New Testament on the other, the underground stream of the people's language springs up powerfully into the daylight. And this colloquial Greek of the early days of Christianity cannot, with truth, be labeled as a "tired" language. Atticism makes a much more tired and senile impression. We can say that it has been a dispensation of Providence that the Apostles have not been Atticists in their sermons, in their letters, and later in their literary productions. For had that been so, Christianity would have been a privileged esoteric affair of a small and exclusive upper class. Because the Apostles spoke the people's language, the Gospel could go among the masses, could start a mission, and could wander from coast to coast.

It is true that, afterward, the Christian Church leagued itself with Atticism. At least, most of the Church Fathers wrote the Greek of the Atticists. And that, naturally, hindered its progress among the masses. But the chief influence among the masses at that time, just as before, was the New Testament, as long as it was kept before their eyes in the pericopes of the public services. This is also true of the Latin New Testament, which is likewise a memorial of the people's speech. It is also quite true of the German and English New Testaments, which strongly reflect the common speech of the Sixteenth Century. Naturally the colloquial languages of the Twentieth Century are somewhat different from those of the Reformation period. Therefore it is only right to translate the New Testament over and over again. It can be truly said that the two great modern attempts to translate the New Testament into English, one by the Scotchman, Dr. James Moffatt, and the other by the American, Dr. Edgar J. Goodspeed, are the after-effects of the revolution in New Testament philology due to referring the New Testament back to the colloquial speech of its period.

* * *

It is very difficult to enter into details within the limits of a short lecture. Therefore I will only just say generally that both the grammar and the lexicography of the New Testament have been revolutionized by the modern methods of New Testament philology, and that the majority of modern commentaries have, to a great extent, adopted the results of the modern investigations, and in some cases they have extended the investigations. We have, already, quite a number of modern grammars of the New Testament. The best in German is the fifth edition of Dr. Friedrich Blass's grammar revised by Dr. Albert Debrunner. The best in English is the still incompleted grammar by my dear and never-to-be-forgotten friend, the late Dr. James Hope Moulton, whose work is continued by Wilbert

THE LANGUAGE 83

Francis Howard. And there is the valuable monster grammar edited by Dr. A. T. Robertson. Just as epoch-making in the realm of lexicography is the work of Moulton and Milligan, *The Vocabulary of the Greek New Testament*, without which the latest and best lexicon in German could not have been made: namely, the new edition of the Dictionary by Dr. Erwin Preuschen, which was recently completed by Dr. Walter Bauer in Göttingen.

To this general statement I will add a few characteristic details in the vocabulary and the syntax.

* * *

With regard to the vocabulary, the usual theory of former times, that the words which are found only in the New Testament were new formations by the Apostles, has been shaken to its foundations. It is true that new words do occur, but in the case of a word which occurs only in the New Testament, it is much safer to take that it is only an accident. For example, Paul used the word λογεία (*logeia*) for the collection which he gathered for the poor Christians in Jerusalem. There was no other instance of this word in the whole of Greek literature. So it was taken for a new formation by the Apostle Paul. But it could be said that a man who made propaganda in order to collect money for a good cause would act very unwisely if he used a brand-new word for his undertaking. And really the facts are these, that the noun λογεία and also the verb λογεύω (*logeuō*), of which no instance had then been found, have been found, in the meantime, not only in Egyptian papyri and ostraca but also in inscriptions in Asia Minor, words which had long been in use among the people and only by an accident did not come up to the literature.

Again, one of the most famous words in the study of the language of the New Testament is ἐπιούσιος (*epiousios*) which occurs in the Lord's Prayer for the word "daily" in "daily bread." This word has been established beyond doubt by the new study. No instance of it occurs in the whole of Greek literature. And besides, the greatest of the old Bible students, Origen, had expressly asserted that the word did not exist before in the Greek language. Years ago I had once taken the risk of doubting this statement of Origen, on the ground that I could not see why it was necessary to coin a new word in this case. The word left to me the impression that it had originated in the everyday life of the people. And I was also guided by the consideration that I myself did not know very many words in the German colloquial language of to-day, and without comparing myself to Origen in any way, it seemed probable to me that he did not know the entire vocabulary of the colloquial language of the First Century A. D. Those experts who believed more in Origen than in modern New Testament philology were taught something better when in a papyrus from the Faijûm, the remains of a housekeeper's book, there appeared, among other requisites, τὰ ἐπιούσια (*ta epiousia*). In the meantime the

Brunn philologist Ferdinand Stiebitz brought the convincing information that this Greek expression τὰ ἐπιούσια corresponded with the Latin expression "diaria," which occurred in a similar list of household requisites in a Latin wall inscription in Pompey. Both words probably signify the amount of daily food given to slaves, soldiers, and laborers, and probably usually allotted a day beforehand. The inscription in Pompey is particularly valuable because it is not later than the time of the origin of the Gospels, being thus almost contemporary with the oldest Greek translation of the Lord's Prayer. The strict meaning of the Prayer is: "Give us to-day our amount of daily food for to-morrow."[1]

In many cases also new light has been thrown by the new discoveries on the special meanings of familiar New Testament words. As an example I will take the word ἀπέχω (*apecho*) from the saying of Jesus in Matthew

---

[1] For further details compare my study, "Noch einmal ἐπιούσιος" in *Reinhold-Seeberg-Festschrift*, Vol. I, Leipzig, 1929, p. 299 ff.

6:2, 5:16, and Luke 6:24: "They have their reward." When it is known from the papyri and the ostraca that the word ἀπέχω is the technical expression regularly used in receipts, the words "they have their reward" in the Sermon on the Mount acquire the more pungent ironical meaning, "They can sign the receipt of their reward." Their right to receive their reward is realized, precisely as if they had given a receipt for it.

I wish to illustrate this example by means of one of those original documents, an ostracon, which comes directly from the time of Jesus Himself, and which is now in my collection of ostraca. It was written two or three years after the Sermon on the Mount, in September or October of the year 32 A. D. It is a receipt for two drachmæ, the alien tax for two months. There, in the second line, you can see the word ἀπέχω quite clearly.[2]

New and better answers have also been

---

[2] The speaker circulated this ostracon (which is published in *Light from the Ancient East*, p. 110 ff.)

found for the grammatical problems. For example, in the familiar passage, which has been a difficult *crux interpretum*, in the Gospel of John 1:14: "and we beheld His Glory; glory as of the only begotten from the Father, full of grace and truth." Here the peculiar "nominative" πλήρης (*pleres*) has been explained in the most peculiar ways. But the papyri teach us that πλήρης had become indeclinable in the time of the New Testament, and perhaps before that. And the despicable potsherds give new instance of its use. An artistic author would naturally have avoided this fossilized πλήρης as a "mistake." That one word πλήρης should be enough to label the Gospel of John as a popular book.

* * *

We must yet deal briefly with an important syntactical question, the question of Hebraisms and general Semitisms in the New Testament. Because the New Testament has been written, for the most part, by native Jews, and, what is more important, because it is influenced in many passages by the Greek translation of the Old Testament through the Septuagint, and, finally, because the sayings of Jesus had been translated from an Aramaic original, it contains, naturally, a number of Semitisms. I have never denied that. What I do deny is this: that the number of these Semitisms is enough to disprove the general view that the New Testament Greek is the colloquial Greek of the period, and to revive the view that it is Jewish Greek, and to call it Greek-Yiddish. The Semitisms only are the birthmarks which show us where primitive Christianity came into existence. But generally regarded, the New Testament is, in spite of its Semitisms, a book of the Mediterranean world, not of the Ghetto.

* * *

The view that the Greek of the New Testament was the language of the common people of its time has given cause, occasionally, to the erroneous opinion that the New Testament was thereby degraded and depreciated. Here I can only confess that to me the New Testament has become greater and more venerable the more I have learned to regard it in close connection with the people of its day. And just from a linguistic standpoint, a consideration of the style of the New Testament shows how important is this little book, created from such simple material, even as a literary document, in the literature of the world.

In this respect a saying of Dante was a great help to me many years ago. It was my good fortune to rediscover it to-day here at Oberlin in the study of one of the greatest living Dante experts, President Wilkins, with the aid of his wonderful Concordance on Dante's Latin writings. Dante, in his book *De vulgari eloquentia*, differentiates within the languages two types: the vulgar, and the artificial or grammatical. And coming to a valuation of these two types he emphasizes with the

THE LANGUAGE 91

genius's intuition the noble superiority of the vulgar language:[3]

> "*Harum quoque duarum nobilior est vulgaris, tum quia prima fuit humano generi usitata, tum quia totus orbis ipsa perfruitur, licet in diversas prolationes et vocabula sit divisa; tum quia naturalis est nobis, cum illa potius artificialis existat.*"

We can summarize the poet's judgment by saying that he prizes the popular language because it is the oldest form of speaking, has prevalence all over the world within the different tongues, and is for us the natural form of expression. By this Dante has given a masterpiece of linguistical insight, which is of a very special importance for the problem before us.

* * *

When I now speak of the style of the New Testament, that does not mean that there is one peculiar New Testament style. The New Testament is a collection of writings by differ-

---
[3] Dante, *De vulgari eloquentia* I, 1, 34 ff. (Tutte le opere di Dante Alighieri, ed. E. Moore, Oxford, 1904, p. 379.)

ent authors, and its style reflects the individuality of the different personalities, whom we must thank for the texts.

And here it should be said that the greatest and most valuable part of the New Testament lies before us not in written style, but in oral style. Both the Master Himself and the greatest of His Apostles spoke their words. Jesus was not a book prophet, and Paul was not an epistle writer. Jesus was the Master of the living word, and Paul also dictated his letters.

With Jesus of Nazareth everything depended on the living word. Although we have in the synoptic sayings of Jesus only fragments of the great treasures of His prophecies, and those fragments are no longer in their original Aramaic language, yet they are quite sufficient to enable us to form a judgment of the peculiarity of the style of these unique lines. Here I venture to make the statement that there is no text so popular as the sayings of Jesus anywhere in the libraries of the world-religions or world-culture. And to the weighty, universal human contents of the Gospel there corresponds the simplest of forms. Simple, great lines join heaven and earth, powerful trumpet sounds arouse the conscience, the everyday facts of human life are the revelations of the Eternal.

When we compare the forms of expression in the prophecies of Jesus with those of human teachers, who stand upon the pinnacle of intellectual literary culture, then the quiet impressiveness of the style of Jesus becomes still clearer. Read a few pages of Plato or a chapter of Kant and then turn again to the Sermon on the Mount or the Parables, and the different types of forms become clear at once.

On the one hand there is the artificial style of speculative thought: long periods in which one becomes quite lost, and finally discovers that the way out of the labyrinth cannot be found. The words of these great thinkers are not understood in the market place, nor would they be understood if anyone spoke them from a fishing boat.

Jesus spoke of the light and the candlestick, of the city on the hill, of father and child, bread and fish, egg and scorpion, of asking and giving, of seed and crop, of hunger and thirst. No long sentences, no speculative questions, everything popular, simple, concise, transparent, pithy, plastic; all this and yet He was never trivial. Although preached on the street corners it was never street-corner wisdom; although clear it was never shallow; never abstract formulations; but always realistic drawings and sketches. The best formal characteristic of Jesus' art of speaking can be given in the word which Winckelmann coined for ancient art, "noble simplicity and calm greatness." On the whole the formal stylistic peculiarity gives to the words of Jesus the character of object lessons. The listener not only hears but also looks and sees, and what is heard and seen remains. That is, the words remain in the minds and souls of simple men, who had never been burdened with learned ballast.

But they also charm the well-educated as expressions which have not been made but have grown. The more one compares the different styles of the great personalities of mankind with one another, the more one realizes that neither the style of Plato nor of Kant was fit for the powerful Gospel message. The Gospel, because it was the message of God to humanity, could only reveal itself in the simplest of garments.

* * *

In clear contrast to the style of the sayings of Jesus is the style of the letters of Paul. When we turn from the Gospels to Paul we pass from the cornfield and the fishing boat to the market place of the big city. While the words of Jesus reflect His rural Galilean home, the language of Paul is saturated with the colors of the Mediterranean emporiums. While the words of Jesus, regarded formally, are the outflow of a simple godly soul, not seldom in the language of Paul we see the vibrations of a very complicated personality.

Because of some complicated passages in the Pauline letters, it is customary, in many circles, to speak of the Paul who is difficult to understand. The difference between the style of Jesus and of Paul is expressed thus: the one is intelligible, the other is unintelligible.

I cannot adopt this comfortable formula. It commits the error of not differentiating in the case of Paul, and we must do so if we wish to understand his style. Already the second Epistle of Peter had differentiated here, when it says of the letters of Paul (probably the author of this Epistle had them already collected before him) that some things in them are "hard to be understood." Moffatt translates "letters containing some knotty points" (II Peter 3:16). Undoubtedly there are long and different sentences in the Pauline letters. In those passages where Paul begins to speculate, where he begins to bring proofs by the dialectic method, naturally he becomes difficult to understand. The ninth, tenth, and eleventh chapters of Romans, taken as a whole, are not easy to understand. The same is true of other parts of the same letter. Because many people begin their acquaintance with Paul with that letter, which now stands, in the Pauline Canon, according to Roman influence, at the beginning, they easily confirm the judgment on Paul that he is difficult to understand.

But that is a misleading generalization. The same Paul who when he speculates often entangles himself in his own net, can find words for his confessions, his exhortations, and his prayers which, in their concise pithiness, remind us of the master words of Jesus. After reading chapters nine to eleven of Romans, go on to chapters twelve to fifteen and chapter sixteen or the thirteenth chapter of first Corinthians, or read quickly through all the Pauline letters, and put together all those passages in which Paul condenses great truths into the shortest space thinkable, in very short sentences of only a few words, in a mottolike, lapidary language. In my book *Paul* I have compared the Apostle, because of his gift of forming plastic banner signs, with Heraclitus, and I believe the comparison is a correct one.

In addition Paul has another gift. He is, up to now, the unequaled master of the liturgical style, which soars high above the dusty street of everyday prose, which, almost in the language of the seer of another world, bears witness to the wonderful secret of that other world. Here the Apostle speaks as a prophet and a psalmist. The classical memorials to this language of Paul are in the letters to the Ephesians and to the Colossians, although the same key is touched occasionally in other letters. It was a grave misunderstanding to take these psalms of the apostolic Christ-cult for Christological and dogmatic treatises and paragraphs.

So we cannot speak of "the" style of Paul because we must distinguish between his different styles. But nothing he says is ever crammed into the artificial forms of Atticism, it is rather created with the simplest means of the popular colloquial language of the ancient city, which he enriched with the language of the Greek Bible—the Septuagint. In all the important matters the language of Paul does not soar far above the heads of the masses. Even to-day the simplest people, and just the simplest people, can understand most of the best of Paul's preaching. And the average man can understand the difficult parts if he is directed by a well-trained theologian. Finally I would advise you to compare Paul, the writer, with other writers of his time. Then you will gain the impression that when the Pauline letters had been collected and reduplicated and so had become a part of literature (contrary to their intention), then the dry regions of the ancient artificial prose, with its rhetorical unreality and its imitation of Attic, were refreshed anew by the stream which came from the depths of the language and souls of the people.

* * *

The task of describing the characteristics of the style of the Johannine texts is easier because we have before us, at least in the Gospel and in the letters of John, a very uniform style. This justifies us in regarding the four texts as belonging together, and having come from the same hand. In the Revelation of John we have, I believe, different styles coming together, the result, chiefly, of the author having used older apocalyptic texts and inserted them in his book. But I think that in quite a number of passages the style which we have known from the Gospel and the letters is to be seen clearly.

The Johannine style is certainly the simplest which we can find in the New Testament. In all matters of form he is quite commonplace (one remembers the word πλήρης (*pleres*) of the prologue.)[4] His vocabulary is not very rich and his syntax is of a quite unequaled simplicity. Those scholars who have called the Gospel of John the philosophical Gospel, or

---
[4]Compare above p. 88.

the Logos Gospel, because they think that the whole book is to be understood from the first lines, come into difficulties when the Gospel is tested by its style. From the stylistic standpoint the book does not look like a philosophical work. From its outward garments and, I believe, also from its content the book was intended for the great mass of Christian believers. For its contents, the great literary synthesis of the old Gospel of Jesus Himself, and of the Christ-cult and Christ-mysticism of the Apostle Paul, found that linguistic form in which the latter, the Pauline Gospel, became the common property of the Church.

It seems to me a mistake to explain the stylistic peculiarity of the Gospel of John and the other Johannine texts as Semitic style. The piling up of principal clauses connected by "and," and the lack of subordinate sentences and long periods, do not in themselves indicate that the author was a Semite. I do not doubt at all that the author was a Semite. But the sentence building in the Johannine texts is not specifically Semitic. Probably it is much more the pre-literary colloquial style of primitive people. I have collected examples of this narrative style from Egyptian papyri, which certainly do not come from Semites, and similar examples can be produced from the popular literature of all nations. I reject the view that the peculiarity of the Johannine style is that of Semitic grammar. Rather I see in the Johannine style an example, perhaps the clearest of the Apostolic popular style.

But I must add one point. This primitive style seems to me to have become already a cult style. Certainly another type of cult style than the Pauline one. But a very impressive style in any case. I can quite understand that the primitive style is the best for the use in the sanctuary. There is a similar style in some fragments belonging to the Isis-cult. Then this liturgical Johannine style regains its own particular spirit when the separate pericopes of the book are read in a divine service, especially when they resound in the semi-darkness of a cathedral, or when they are chanted or psalmodized. For this book was intended for the divine services. The evangelist, when he wrote, inserted much in his book that he had not created just when he wrote it, but which he had created previously and had read many times previously in the divine services.

Finally, I think it can be proved without difficulty that to-day this great book of the people, the Gospel of John, is far from being un-understandable among Christian people. For this I have collected a great deal of material from literature, from my own observations, from information given by clergy friends at home, and from the mission fields. And I may ask you yourselves to observe again to what extent the words of John and the Johannine pericopes are appreciated and are living among the lowly. Here again it is confirmed that the texts of the New Testament have human character, not only intelligible to a small circle of esoterics, but also sinking into the souls of the unknown and the forgotten of the world.

* * *

But there is also much to be said about the style of the other New Testament writers. The time being so short, I must confine myself to a very few sentences concerning Luke and the Catholic Epistles. The Synoptic Evangelists, because they, for the most part, only repeated the tradition about Jesus, as a rule did not have opportunity to show their own peculiarities of style. Only Luke, who added to his Gospel a second book, the Acts of the Apostles, appears to us as a stylist. We notice that he makes a closer approach to a literary form than the other evangelists. In particular his vocabulary is more refined than that of the others, and on the whole we are on a higher plane when we read him. But we do not leave the native class of the New Testament. Luke also, with his gift for plastic form, stands before us as a prominent popular narrator.

Of the Catholic Epistles, that of James belongs in the matter of style with the Synoptic Gospels, while those of Jude and Peter are nearer to Paul.

But we enter another world when we open the Epistle to the Hebrews. Here I can only repeat what I have already said in a previous lecture. The Epistle to the Hebrews seems to me to be the first clear product of early Christian artificial prose. With it Early Christianity first stepped out of its native land and began to climb to the level of high literary culture.

* * *

Whoever has eyes to see can learn much from the linguistic facts which meet us in the New Testament. The linguistic estimation of the New Testament shows us that our Holy Book in its classical, creative period is in close contact with the middle and lower classes and in sharp contrast to the old artificial Atticistic culture which struggled for a new lease of life in the surrounding world. Had the Gospel leagued itself with this ancient culture from the beginning it would have endangered what is best in it, and, especially, its future as a message to humanity would have been impossible.

This complicated Atticistic culture was something only for the few. The masses craved for the simple, and the divine revelation of the Gospel demanded a plain garb. The complicated is immobile, the simple is mobile. The New Testament, as is proved also by its language, was ordained for a destiny, the like of which no work which originated in the high literary culture has had, or could have had. Let us remember Dante: "*Nobilior est vulgaris eloquentia . . . totus orbis ipsa perfruitur.*" This simple book, with its carpenter's and tent maker's language, was a book for all, and it could resound, unadulterated to humanity in all centuries, the message of the Gospel which had moved men in a small corner of the Mediterranean world.

IV

THE NEW TESTAMENT IN WORLD HISTORY

IV

THE NEW TESTAMENT IN WORLD HISTORY

EARLY Christianity, which originated in a world of writing and books, had nothing to do with books. Neither Jesus nor Paul took up the pen to preserve their teaching for posterity. Jesus never wrote a word for literary purposes. Paul wrote non-literary letters to certain fellow believers when occasion demanded; he never thought of creating Christian literature for future generations. But it was the good pleasure of God to give to the revelations of the Master and the confessions of His Apostle an unparalleled position in World History.

The main clear lines of the creative period of our religion do not run from the higher to the lower, but rather upward from the lower to the higher. Like a spring from the hidden depths the Gospel bubbles up from the soul of the people's prophet of Nazareth. Jesus was not a book prophet, neither was He an academic founder of religion. And the papyrus sheets of the letters of Paul did not pride themselves on being pretentious pamphlets for the universities of Alexandria or Athens. They were not on the book market for the educated; they went modestly out of the workshop of an unknown tent maker to the unknown of the big cities of the Mediterranean world. But to-day the Gospels and the Pauline letters, together with the literary products of the second period of the Apostolic age, form the Book of Humanity.

The Early Church accomplished a deed of unique historical importance when it saved the remains of Jesus and His Apostles and collected them in the New Testament.

We call the New Testament the Book of Humanity because of its contents. It contains information concerning the most powerful spiritual movement of mankind in the history of the world. But the New Testament appears to us as the Book of Humanity especially on account of its world-wide history during nearly two thousand years. "*Habent sua fata libelli*": books have their destinies. How much could be said of the *fata* of books! But there does not exist a single book in the whole, immense library of mankind whose *fata* come anywhere near being as extensive and intensive as those of the New Testament.

We will consider this world-wide history and find out the way over which the New Testament has traveled during all those centuries.

* * *

The first highroad of the New Testament is the one leading out of obscurity into the big wide world. Here a wonderful picture unfolds before our eyes. Just as we see the Master's profound parable of the mustard seed in the history of Christianity in general, so also we can see it fulfilled in the history of the New Testament.

As late as the middle of the Second Century, a hundred years after the time of Paul, the Gospels, the Acts of the Apostles, and the letters of Paul—the groundwork of the Canon—lay in the obscurity of the Christian brotherhoods in the emporiums of the Mediterranean coastlands. Compared with its position in the year 70 or 100 A. D., Christianity shows a steady progress in the number of souls and communities. But compared with the great spiritual powers of the surrounding world Christianity was small and hardly noticed. The number of copies of the Holy Scriptures of the New Testament would amount perhaps to a few hundred. Every Christian did not possess a copy of the Gospel. As a rule, the local churches would have one or two copies. No part of an original manuscript of the New Testament belonging to this period has come down to us. Probably we would have Second Century fragments of the New Testament if Christianity had reached Egypt in the early period.

But a hundred years later, in the Third Century A. D., in the age of the Christian persecutions, the position is quite different. At that time there were probably thousands of copies of the Gospels or of the whole New Testament in circulation, and hundreds of them were given up to the authorities by renegade Christians and destroyed. The New Testament was already a power in the life of the public, and with irresistible triumph it had settled in all parts of the Greek-speaking world. We have small original fragments of the Greek Bible belonging to this period on pieces of papyrus from Egypt. The small Exodus fragment I showed you[1] may give you an idea of the appearance of a Gospel sheet of that period.

A hundred years later, about the middle of the Fourth Century, after Christianity had conquered the ancient world, the number of

[1] A Third Century fragment from the speaker's collection.

copies of the New Testament had increased considerably. From this and the following century we have entire manuscripts, richly ornamented; they are the priceless possessions of the libraries in the Vatican, in the British Museum, and in Leningrad.

Although the Eastern Mediterranean lands were overrun by Islam, and many old churches containing copies of the Bible were destroyed, yet we have to-day more manuscripts of the Greek New Testament, written from the Fourth to the Fifteenth Century and later, than of any other book of the ancient world.

The number of the manuscripts of the Greek New Testament, or of parts of it, which are known up to date, is about forty-six hundred, including the New Testament commentaries of the Church Fathers. This number is not yet closed. Whoever travels in the East with his eyes open will perhaps occasionally find new Biblical parchments. During the last twenty-three years I myself have seen about twelve to fifteen previously unknown parchment manuscripts of the New Testament or of parts of it. Last fall I discovered some in secret Turkish libraries and in Bulgaria. Previous to that time I acquired some for European and American libraries, the last in 1927, a Greek Tetra-Evangelium (a Four Gospel Book) from Asia Minor, which is now in the Library of the Southern Baptist Theological Seminary in Louisville, Kentucky. In 1928, in the *Zeitschrift fuer Neutestamentliche Wissenschaft* Professor von Dobschuetz of the University of Halle gave a list of recently discovered New Testament manuscripts including this Louisville copy. But one could now supplement this list considerably. I am glad to show you some white and black photos of two Greek Gospel-codices of those I found last fall: the first two photos show the first pages of St. Matthew and St. Mark, the third gives a picture of the index of pericopes on page 498 of the first codex; the fourth photo shows the first page of St. Mark in the other codex.

* * *

While the New Testament marched victoriously over the wide territory of the ancient Greek world, that is, over parts of Syria, Asia Minor, Greece, parts of Italy and Gaul and Egypt, at the same time it entered other territories where other languages were spoken. The Greek Holy Book came next to its Eastern home, to the Syrians, the Copts, Ethiopians, Arabs, Armenians, and other Orientals, and soon it was dressed in the curious garments of all these languages. The history of the Syriac and Coptic translations of the New Testament alone is such a comprehensive chapter that it takes the coöperation of many experts to recount it.

But the Holy Book conquered the West as well. In the language of the West, as the Latin Bible, it exercised its peculiar historical influence for centuries, from Tertullian and Cyprian to Hieronymus and Augustine in North Africa and the southwestern lands of Europe, and then through the Middle Ages in the whole wide territory of the Roman Church. We can distinguish two Latin translations: the

Old Latin, the so-called Itala, and the later, the so-called Vulgate of Hieronymus, which is really a revision of the Itala. Here again the numbers of the preserved manuscripts reflect the noble destiny of our Holy Book. Only a comparatively small number of manuscripts exist of the Itala, which was gradually supplanted by the Vulgate of Hieronymus, but these few are jewels of the first rank. Of the Latin Bible of Hieronymus there are, however, well over eight thousand parchment manuscripts, which have been catalogued. To the interesting question, why the number of the Latin codices is nearly twice that of the Greek, the answer is that the Greek manuscripts in the East were destroyed by thousands by the neverending invasions, while there was no such destruction in the West. Unfortunately, the events of the last decades again have destroyed a number of Greek manuscripts in the East.

The Latin New Testament is also written in the language of the people. Yet it can be said that through the genius of the Latin language our Holy Book was put on a somewhat different plane from that of the original Greek text. The Latin New Testament shows an aristocratic character in some points, and often a change into a grandiloquent lapidary style. On the whole it is a Westernized book, a new Bible, as is the case with every great translation of the Bible, beginning with the Septuagint down to the Bible of Luther and the English translations. In the numerous Romanic translations the New Testament sets out on its victorious march through the West. But the New Testament began also to conquer the soul of the North-European peoples. Already a beginning had been made in the Fourth Century with the Gothic Bible of Ulfilas, which originated in the southeast of Europe. This was the first Germanic Bible. And now from the Ninth Century onward there followed the Slavonic translations. I can show you a photo of an Old-Slavonic Evangeliarium of the Fifteenth Century which I found in a Turkish library last fall; the page contains

Matthew 5:18–22 (Sermon on the Mount). Later in the Middle Ages we see the beginnings of the Scandinavian and the Celtic translations.

* * *

Two modern Western translations of the Bible have come to be regarded more and more as World Bibles, the German Bible translated by Luther and the English Bible.

There were already a number of German translations in the late Middle Ages, but these were soon forgotten when there appeared the most influential translation which a book has ever had on the European Continent, Luther's German New Testament. With Luther's translation we have reached one of the most important epochs in the world-wide history of the New Testament since the time of its origin.

Luther made the New Testament again the book of the people, and the new art of printing gave to the powerful spiritual force which he set free in the people an unparalleled means of circulation.

Printing press and Reformation signify machine and soul, or technical art and religion. Each of these forces presses to subdue the world. Both of them, technical art and religion, leagued together could subdue the world, that world which underwent at the same time so great a change. It was no longer the small ancient world, half of which spiritually belonged to the Pope and the other half subject to the Turk, but the new big world, conquered by discoverers and explorers, and again settled by brave pioneers whose imagination was excited by its wonders.

For the march through this big world the New Testament put on the garment of the English language. While Luther's Bible had directly and indirectly the greatest influence in Christian Europe, the English Bible, although influenced by Luther, became the World Bible in the modern sense of the word. With the colonists who settled in the New World the New Testament traveled far over the ocean.

Then as the world missions grew with the increase of international communication during the last two centuries, the New Testament experienced a new era in its history through innumerable new translations. Here especially the English-speaking Christendom rendered great service. The British and Foreign Bible Society has, during the century and a quarter of its existence, guided the destiny of the New Testament in a way of which Luther could not have dreamed.

When the British and Foreign Bible Society was founded in 1804 the Bible or parts of it were translated into a little over 60 languages. In 1921 the number of the languages in which the Society translated, printed, and circulated the Bible or parts of it had increased from 60 to 543, in 1927 to 590, in 1928 to 609, on May 1, 1929, to 618. The Society's well-known small volume entitled "The Gospel in Many Tongues" gives the words of John 3:16 ("For God so loved the world"), or in a few exceptions some other verse, in those 590 languages. Within very narrow limits this volume offers to us an instructive view which fills us with awe of the *fata* of the Book of Books among mankind. The progress of the Gospel through the centuries and among the nations can hardly be presented in a better way to the Christian Church and especially to the young than by means of this little book with its over sixty different types. If we include the translations circulated by other societies, we would have to count over 840 languages or dialects in which the Bible or parts of it are translated to-day.

The number of copies that are circulated is correspondingly great. The British and Foreign Bible Society had circulated about 375,000,000 copies of the Bible or parts thereof up to 1928, the annual figure of 1928 being about 11,400,000 volumes.

To this number must be added the figures of other Bible and missionary societies and also those of private publishers, and we have an inestimable number of the polyglot circulation of the Bible. The American Bible Society, for example, had circulated since its beginning in 1816 up to 1928 about 205,000,000 copies, the annual figure of 1928 being about 11,000,000. Naturally, the New Testament has the foremost place in these numbers.

* * *

The New Testament is found to-day wherever the foot of a European or American goes; it has reached farther than gunpowder, and the mileage it has traveled cannot be equaled by any railway track. Finally modern science has enabled us to send the words of the New Testament round the world on ether waves, and has thus increased greatly the means of spreading its force. We can say confidently that neither the Holy Scriptures of Islam nor those of Buddhism nor the masterpieces of the great poets of any people have the same position in the world as the New Testament.[2]

---

[2] According to *Ev. Kirchenblatt* (Posen), March, 1929, The Soviet-Russian publishers, during the last ten years, have circulated about 13,000,000 volumes of the works of Lenin in 36 languages.

Whoever takes active part in the study of the New Testament receives daily proof of its unique position in mankind. A few personal experiences which I have had closely following one another will serve by way of illustration. Years ago I learned of the transactions concerning a translation of the New Testament into Kaschgar. At the same time I heard that an English translation of a German book on the New Testament had been ordered from a London publisher, not only by numerous buyers in America and Canada, but also by individuals in China, Tokyo, and Mombasa. The Kaschgar New Testament is intended for the interior of Central Asia. The other names lead us from America to the Far East and East Africa. In the same week a member of my New Testament Seminar in Berlin brought back to me an Oriental manuscript of the Gospels of the Eleventh Century which belongs to the Seminar. The young scholar had worked for months making a close comparison of it. And so he added to the impressions of the modern history of the New Testament a glimpse into a part of its history in the Middle Ages.

* * *

This is the first highroad of the New Testament in its unparalleled history: the way out of the obscurity into the big, wide world.

The other path of the little book is conditioned by the first. It is the way leading from its native class of simple people up into the classes of the educated, those of literary culture and worldly power.

This course of the New Testament is perhaps still more interesting than the first. The first way has long been accurately described and surveyed, but very little consideration has been given to the second. Its history must yet be written, and it is a very rich history. For the ascent of the New Testament is one of the great chapters in the history of man's culture.

The ascent of the New Testament! The simple book which came from the souls of blessed, simple men has always remained the possession of the simple. And in the lean times of Christianity the spiritual value of the New Testament was securely held in the souls of the Christian people. But this living force also pushed upward. And thus we see the vital sap moving upward from the roots to the trunk and to the twisted branches of human culture.

We have a valuable document belonging to the Second Century which shows us the New Testament still in the midst of its native class: it is the list of the books of the Canon, which I have already mentioned. It is written in a very vulgar Latin, the peculiarities of which should not be "corrected." That is typical: the same hard and crooked hands which received the Holy Book in the simple assembly rooms of the post-Apostolic times still hold it tightly as their own possession. It is not yet the domain of the theologian.

Nevertheless, in the middle of the Second Century the New Testament, at least its chief constituent parts, was in the hands of the learned. The Christian scribes began to deal with the New Testament much in the same way as the rabbis dealt with the Old Testament and the grammarians with the classical literature. Soon work had commenced on the text and on the interpretation. A *bibliotheca sacra* of commentaries and sermons came into existence. Nearly all the Church Fathers were Bible students in their way. During the Middle Ages the work was continued not so much in producing as in reproducing.

The exegetical work of the Reformation was creative for the intuitive conception of the motive forces of the New Testament. This creative work was continued in the historical and philological spheres during the Seventeenth and Eighteenth centuries. We stand to-day on the shoulders both of the Reformers and of the fathers of the modern historical and philological methods. To-day the New Testament is one of the greatest subjects of expert scholarship in the colleges and universities all over the world. There are, perhaps, four or five hundred academic chairs for the study of the

New Testament at about three hundred different places in the world. The number of the experts who coöperate in the study of the New Testament is considerably greater; among them there are many philologists and some excellent women scholars.

* * *

Undoubtedly this ascent from the mind of the simple people to the intellect of the learned meant a great danger to the New Testament; the same danger which there is for the anemone of the Galilean spring when a learned man with a green botanizing box plucks it out and puts it in an herbarium; the same danger which there is for the olive tree of Anatolia when it is transplanted to Tübingen or Berlin.

Often enough the little book has been threatened by this danger. It has seemed as if oceans of ink would drown it, clouds of dust suffocate it, and mountains of paper bury it. Even in the modern study of the Bible there is still prevalent on the right and left a strange doctrinaire method of considering and estimating the New Testament, a method which is interested primarily in the so-called "theology" of the Holy Book. This method formed a theological teaching from the flowing and ebbing religious life of the New Testament. From the spirit of the first witnesses it makes a law, from the personalities of Jesus and His Apostles, systems, from Paul a Paulinism, and from Christ a Christology.

Consequently we often get a distorted and lifeless picture of Early Christianity. Everything is dogmatized and conventionalized; much is fossilized and darkened; and the connection with the deep mystic soul of the East is destroyed. These experiences of the New Testament belong to the gloom chapters of its history. That which came from the mind of prophets in the sunny East, in the open air and free sunlight, feels as if it were in exile on the wooden tables under the Osram lamps of the Western authorities.

On the other hand, many a time scholarly study has been the pathmaker into the heart of the little Book and opened new ways which it should go through the labyrinth of polyglot mankind. Luther coined a fine word and Goethe borrowed it from the Reformer:

*"Die alten Sprachen sind die Scheiden,
 Darinnen das Messer des Geistes steckt."*

("The old tongues are the sheaths in which the knife of the spirit is put.") That is the value of scholarly study of the Bible: that it knows how to restore the original text and how to interpret the "*Urtext*"; that it leads back to the very sources, linguistical as well as historical; that it trains every new generation of students to sharpen that "knife of the spirit," and that it protects the Holy Book from the violence of the confused thinkers, the fanatics, the timid, and the legalists. May it more and more lead to repentance even those prodigal commentators who do not ask: "What does Jesus say?" or "What is St. Paul's opinion?" but rather like to emphasize what they would say if they were Christ or if they would write to the Romans!

* * *

The ascent of the New Testament into the sphere of learning was thus both a danger to the little Book and a protection.

But with that we have touched upon only a part of the destinies of the ascending New Testament. We must add some remarks about the world-wide influence which it has had in all spheres of spiritual culture.

I am thinking of the way in which fine art has been enriched by our Holy Book. In the earliest times it was still the simple art of people which was congenial to the nature of the New Testament, art which was stimulated in particular by the Gospels. There are the primitive popular drawings of the old Christian catacombs, with their plain material, their simple lines, and their naïve conceptions.

Then came the period of the marble reliefs and sarcophagi and the elaborate frescos up to the classical art of the Renaissance, whose aristocratically dressed Evangelists, pompously draped Areopagus-Pauls, and adorned Madonnas are often quite strange to the New Testament. On the other hand, Dürer and Rembrandt reincarnated spirit from the spirit of the New Testament, and Johann Sebastian Bach is often, from purely artistic intuition, a better interpreter of the Passion than the Passion writers and the Passion preachers.

Less noticed, but really great in its influence, is the impulse which the New Testament gave to the Law. Marriage law, criminal law, public and civil law, were influenced alike in many important points by the New Testament ideas. The leaders in political and social campaigns have, often enough, sharpened their weapons on the New Testament. And even when political hypocrites made their bad use of the New Testament slogans they gave evidence to the majesty of our Holy Book.

An important instance of the influence of the little Book on the culture of mankind is the enriching of the languages with the words and metaphors of the New Testament. In addition to Shakespeare and Goethe, whose language is saturated with the New Testament, there might be mentioned nearly all poets in the literature of the Christian world. The orators in Parliaments, the great journalists, indeed all of us in our everyday language, stand under this formal influence of the spiritual eminence to which the New Testament ascended from the obscurity of its origin.

But the deepest influence of the New Testament, and therefore the most wonderful of its destinies, is seen in its own sphere, in the spiritual, in the religious life of humanity, and especially in the religious life of the Church itself. The history of the missions, home missions as well as foreign missions, is mainly the history of the influence of the New Testament. The history of the Church in all its great periods, where in darkness a new light has shone forth, and where in weakness a new strength has been found, is the history of the influence of the New Testament. Whether it is the story of the Christian martyrs up to the Massacred Witnesses and the Baltic victims or the rediscovery of grace by St. Augustine, the mysticism of the Eastern and Western Catholic Churches and the Christlike life of St. Francis, or the Burning Bush of the Reformation or the building up of the New World through the Pilgrim Fathers, or the modern social and ecumenical movements of Christianity, all of these are unthinkable without the New Testament.

But greater, perhaps, than the influence in all these different spheres accessible to historical investigation is that which no historian can record: the influence of the New Testament upon millions and millions of simple souls during nearly two thousand years of its history. That the New Testament has conquered the wide territory of human culture, that it, through great leaders, has created epochs in the history of the Church, these facts confirmed by history must yet retreat behind the inferred fact that the New Testament, returning home again and again, has conquered the individual human soul of the unknown.

"Has conquered" here means: "brought into fellowship with the living Christ and through Him with the living God," it means submission to the living Christ and to the living God, it means forgiveness of sins and reconciliation, it means transmission of the power of eternal life.

All these effects of the New Testament inaccessible to History are mighty in the Kingdom of God. St. Augustine's distress, Luther's struggle for salvation, Wesley's conversion, are culminating points visible from afar in the daylight of History. The secret effects which no eye has seen and no ear heard are greater.

❋ ❋ ❋

This survey of the New Testament in World History permits us to call the Book that was originally the simple Book of the People, the Great Book of the Peoples. Along the two ways which it has taken through the centuries the New Testament has become the Book of the Peoples. And these two ways, the way from obscurity out into the wide world, and the way from the depths of unliterary folk up to the heights of academical culture, would not have been possible had it been the artificial product of ancient learned study.

Therefore we can put the wonderful history of the Book of Humanity in one sentence: the New Testament has become the Book of the Peoples because it began by being the Book of the People.

V

THE HISTORICAL VALUE OF THE NEW TESTAMENT

V

THE HISTORICAL VALUE OF THE NEW TESTAMENT

THE New Testament has a double character: it is a collection of the written memorials of Early Christianity, and it is the Holy Book of Christianity to-day; it is handed down to us in a dead language, and it is translated to-day into hundreds of living languages; it is put in our libraries, and it is laid on our altars; it is the object of the minute criticisms of experts, and it satisfies hungry souls; it is a mine of historical information, and it is a source of religious power; it is of the past, and it is also of the present.

Because of this double character of the New Testament the question with which we shall deal in the last two lectures has also a double aspect. We shall inquire into the historical value of the New Testament and also into its religious value. We shall thus test its historical reliability, and we shall think of its religious significance for us to-day.

* * *

I cannot, within the limits of this lecture, plunge into the important question whether or not the religious value of a Biblical text depends on the results of historical criticism. It may be sufficient to-day to say that I personally do not think that history is the basis of the holy. I become more and more convinced of the primacy and the autonomy of the holy.

Therefore I am of the opinion that we should not overestimate the bearing of historical investigation upon the religious valuation of the New Testament. But this does not mean, of course, any depreciation of the subject of this lecture itself. The problem of the historical value of the New Testament is certainly one of the greatest problems of modern theology.

* * *

HISTORICAL VALUE

Now my attitude toward the problem of the historical reliability of the New Testament is strongly influenced by two considerations, which appear to me more and more important, and which have been part of the background of my theological work. I explained them in the previous lectures. First I have emphasized that the New Testament contains a great number of texts which are non-literary in character, especially the Pauline letters; and secondly that the great majority of the New Testament texts are of a more or less popular character. Many liberal and conservative critics have treated the letters of Paul as if they were literary compositions, and have treated the New Testament as a whole as a collection of more or less theological art productions.

In particular the popular character of the Gospels has not been recognized by many people. They have treated these popular books as the product of certain theological tendencies. There are eccentric persons to be found who regard the Gospels as the inventions of anonymous authors of the Imperial period, and deny the historicity of Jesus.

It is remarkable that in these problems of religious history the eccentrics and the dilettantes have such a great number of adherents. Long before Arthur Drews, the statement "Jesus has not existed" belonged to the standing stock of agitators, especially in European labor circles. The argument is always the same; if Jesus had really existed, the pagan historians of the Roman Imperial period must have mentioned Him; there must be non-Christian accounts in addition to the Gospel traditions; the Christian traditions alone have no value.

Now we can say first of all that Jesus has not been ignored by pagan authors. He is also mentioned in the old Jewish texts, and, besides the Gospels, we have a quite different group of early Christian sources; especially the letters of Paul. But for my part I would answer these objections with reference to the fact that Early

Christianity was a religious movement among the lower classes, at first a small hidden mustard seed. The men of literature, on the whole aristocratic, had they noticed it in the period of its beginnings, would not have mentioned it, regarding it as a despicable, proletarian movement. But, as a rule, they did not even notice it in the time of its beginnings.

Thus the fact that even later on Early Christianity was only seldom mentioned by pagan authors is simply due to its social structure. The Gospels are not quoted in the Græco-Roman literature just because these thin, modest little books were never found on the bookstalls of the capitals, but, like a kind of secret literature, they were hidden in the houses of those unknown people who with a few exceptions composed the Christian brotherhoods. Anatole France in one of his narratives has with the poet's intuition fully recognized this fact.

With reference to the social structure of

Early Christianity as it is still reflected clearly in the language of the Greek Gospels, we must add that it is as unthinkable that what we call Jesus and Early Christianity came up from these circles automatically, as that Christianity was invented in one of the studies of the ancient world. It is easy to understand that the religious movement of the Gospel was rooted among the lower classes; but that it originated of itself among the anonymous men of these classes, and that afterward the name "Jesus" was affixed to it like a mummy label is unbelievable. For the historian it is only natural that behind this magnificent religious development there lay a power, the power of a great religious personality.

* * *

But on this account we must observe carefully the Gospel tradition and see whether it justifies our faith in it. For this purpose, in agreement with the great majority of scholars from all countries, I distinguish the first three Gospels, the Synoptic Gospels of Matthew, Mark, and

Luke, as a special group from the Fourth Gospel of John, and I will consider each of these groups separately.

How far are the Synoptic Gospels historically reliable? We must not be prejudiced against the historical value of the Synoptic Gospels just because we are not absolutely certain of the authors nor of the year they were composed, or because certain other questions relative to their origin must be left open. For the estimation of the historical value of the tradition of the words and work of Jesus it is not essential to know whether they were recorded by an Apostle or by another Christian, or to know whether they were written in 40 or in 60 A. D. It depends entirely on whether the inner probability of their whole character and of the details merit our belief in them.

The external evidence compared with that of many other ancient historical texts is certainly very good. Last winter in our Berlin Greek Society called "Græca" we began to study Arrian's *Anabasis* of Alexander the Great, and Dr. Ulrich Wilcken gave us a fine introduction, especially examining the question of the sources used by Arrian, who wrote in the Second Century A. D. Then I was deeply impressed by the fact that between Alexander and the writing of those of his biographies which are still in our hands there lies a very long interval, all contemporary biographers being lost and only accessible to us by occasional quotations in later books.

Compared with these conditions of the Alexander tradition the Jesus tradition is very near to the facts themselves. From an originally oral tradition which later became fixed in writing, the Synoptic Gospels were composed in their present form about a generation after the death of Jesus. That we deal here with the tradition of the community does not detract from its value, for all traditions concerning spiritual movements are in their oldest forms traditions of the adherents, traditions of the respective communities. And the nature of the

HISTORICAL VALUE

personality of a founder of a community can be best ascertained from his followers.

* * *

But although the external facts are so favorable, it must be said that the historical value of the Synoptic Gospels can only be ascertained through internal criticism. Internal criticism is always difficult, and its secret is only revealed to the expert who has spent long years on the investigation of the sources. Although internal criticism strives for objective facts, yet it must be borne in mind that there is in it always a subjective element, and it must always be conscious of the relativity of historical knowledge.

Our critical conclusion will not be based on general hypotheses of the circumstances of the origin of the Synoptic Gospels. It is not advisable to form a general and hasty conclusion. It must be a conclusion formed from close investigation of each single part. I certainly accept the theory that the Gospel of Mark is the earliest of the preserved Gospels and that the authors of the other two Synoptic Gospels used beside that of Mark one or more records which were composed chiefly of the sayings of Jesus. But I cannot make a definite decision and say that this one or that one of the three Synoptic Gospels as such contains the best tradition. I would not take the early date of the Gospel of Mark as a reason for regarding in all cases its tradition as the most reliable. I would rather consider that not only the single pericopes, but also the single sayings of Jesus have had their own separate history in the oral and written tradition, and I believe that the chief task of the Synoptic study is to ascertain which of these separate traditional texts of the pericopes appears to be the primary. This method may be called "synoptic eclecticism." I think Johannes Weiss coined the word. To be sure, it is not a beautiful title but it signifies what I hold to be correct. I consider the whole tradition of the Synoptics as one coherent group of ancient texts, which was handed down with many variants, and I believe it can be said

HISTORICAL VALUE

that in many cases it is possible to work back from a tertiary and secondary text to a primary tradition, to an "*Urtext.*"

In the critical testing, especially of the several sayings of Jesus, attention should be given to the following possibilities:

1. That the tradition is intact and trustworthy;
2. That in the course of time it has been shortened, expanded, or altered in some way or other; namely, either through mere accident during its eventful history, or through the temper of popular religion, or through unconscious or conscious adaptation to the requirements of the Apostolic Christ-cult.

In many cases even a hasty comparison of the variants of a certain passage will show clear traces of the alteration of the original due to one or more of the causes enumerated.

In the attempt to solve the problem which of the different traditions is the primary we must dismiss all doctrinaire presuppositions. In particular, with the sayings of Jesus we must be on our guard against suspecting the peculiar and the paradoxical. Those sayings of Jesus which disconcert the commonplace intelligence of the dilettante by their paradoxes prove in the proper psychological test to be genuine.

When Julius Wellhausen belittled the historicity of the collection of sayings of Jesus (the so-called source "Q") and in that way the historical value of the Gospels of Luke and Matthew as compared with that of Mark, because a considerable part of the material was the deposit of the beliefs of the community, he overrated the trustworthiness of his own method of historical and literary criticism and underrated the ability of the community to inform itself concerning its own origin. When other scholars, denying the historicity of Jesus, declare that the Synoptic sayings of Jesus hang in the air, and attribute them to an unknown man, in an uncertain period, in unknown circumstances, strictly all they have done is to erase the *nomen proprium* Ἰησοῦς from the tradition. But even if the name is erased the facts remain and behind them the creative personality. Then we must discover the creative power which we hitherto called Jesus in this or in that unknown. To make the sayings of Jesus anonymous, which is the characteristic of this hypothesis, does not help in any way to solve the historical problems. It only puts the Synoptic problem or part of it into the utmost darkness, into a company of anonymous prophets, thinkers, and poets, a community of unknown men in an unknown place in an unknown period, wholly inaccessible to the investigator.

The fact ascertained by sane investigation, bewailed by the faint-hearted, disputed by apologists and ridiculed by unbelief, the fact that our earliest tradition of Jesus, the Synoptic tradition, often divides into two or three branches, is for a calm historical judgment an argument for authenticity of the greatest importance. There must be a theme behind the variants and the theme depends on a master who created it. A sensitive internal criticism of the variants enables us very often to ascertain the early stages of the variation, and to work back from the variation to the theme and to the Master.

If I am allowed to indicate my general conclusion, attained through many years of work, it is this: The Synoptic Gospels are great treasure houses with a rich abundance of genuine reminiscences of Jesus. Side by side with the genuine there are others whose genuineness is doubtful or denied. But even those pictures of Christ which were created by the sincere art of His disciples have their value as memorials of the Apostolic Christ-cult and are therefore evidence for the powerful influence of the personality of Christ on His followers.

Summing up: we cannot regard the Synoptic Gospels as one homogeneous group of the same historical value, we must not overlook the different strata. Tertiary and secondary strata

HISTORICAL VALUE

lay over the primary. But the primary can be ascertained in many cases.

* * *

Through the entire stratification runs the golden vein of the sayings of Jesus. The fact that the Synoptic tradition is also a tradition of miracles does not detract from the historical value of its tradition. That the Gospels are not merely a collection of sayings but also narratives of miracles was an historical necessity. The Roman historians of the same period not only give accounts of miracles which in their contents are much more grotesque than those of the Gospels, but they were themselves believers in miracles: Livy, Tacitus, and, still more, Suetonius. It would have been astonishing and even suspicious if no richly colored pictures of the marvelous works of the Saviour had been included in the Gospel texts, in books whose existence is due to the requirements of the Apostolic Christ-cult.

Each miracle account of the Synoptics requires special investigation. But when a number of these miracle stories are regarded for strong reasons as secondary, that does not detract from the historical value of the tradition of the Synoptics as a whole.

Here it is necessary to lay particular emphasis on one fact: among the hundreds of sayings of Jesus which have been preserved by the Synoptic Evangelists only a very small number is organically connected with a miracle account, either as preparation for a miracle, or as the result of a miracle, or referring to a past miracle. Thus the tradition of the sayings is very loosely connected with the tradition of miracles, and criticism of the one does not necessarily affect the other.

Using the modern terminology of the historical method, the Synoptic tradition as a whole contains both remains of the history of Jesus and tradition of the history of Jesus. By remains, we are to understand those parts which have remained comparatively unaltered. In the very first rank are those sayings of Jesus which have been preserved in the original

Aramaic. But practically we can add the great majority of the sayings of Jesus in Greek. Besides the remains are the traditions. By tradition, we mean a more or less subjective information about Jesus. On the whole the remains, in the narrow or in the wide sense of the word, seem to me to occupy the foreground in the Synoptic texts.

The remains of the history of Jesus, in particular the many genuine words of Jesus which we have in the Synoptics, are, it is true, not sufficient to form a biography, but they give us the main outlines of His character, His inner life; and I believe that it is far more important for us to know the soul of Jesus than to know the succession of the external facts of his life.

* * *

The Gospel of John is much more of a book of cult confessions than the first three Gospels. It gives, for example, to the sayings and the miracles a much closer mutual connection than they have in the Synoptics. In the Fourth Gospel the miracle very often is but the starting point for great revelations of higher things. As I said before, I am convinced it is the work of a personal disciple of Jesus, who later came under the predominant influence of Pauline Christ-mysticism and Pauline Christ-cult. He gained a wealth of deep experiences of Christ through a long life lived in spiritual fellowship with the exalted Christ. This spiritual experience of Christ and his own recollections, probably strengthened by the knowledge of the Synoptic Gospels, formed one organic unity. Thus his Gospel revealed to the churches both recollections of Jesus and the power of Christ.

What is the significance of these facts for the historical value of the Gospel of John? If we again employ the distinction between remains and tradition, we can say: although remains of the history of Jesus are not wanting altogether in the Gospel of John, yet it is cult-tradition, transmitted through the medium of the personality of the author, which composes the greater part of the Johannine texts. As a book of cult confessions the Gospel of John is a source of first-rate importance for the history of Apostolic Christianity. But it is also of great value for the history of Jesus. Firstly, in those parts which are to be regarded as remains, and secondly, as a peculiar indirect source. The Gospel of John also indicates the great influence of the historical personality of Jesus on the Apostolic Church, and even where it contains no remains we see behind the Christ-confessions the historical personality of Jesus.

* * *

The Acts of the Apostles has also a double character. Here also there is incorporated material which came from the author's own memory; namely, the so-called "We"-narratives, and those which were familiar to him of the Apostolic tradition. The historical value of this last material is considerable, although Luke is not a critical historian in the modern sense of the word. But his own recollections are of an extraordinary value, not only for the history of Early Christianity but also for the history of culture in the Roman Imperial period. Because Luke himself did not stand in the midst of the events, but was only a collaborator of Paul in some periods and scenes, he is to be corrected in some of his accounts from the letters of Paul. He did not know the contents of the Pauline letters; they were still unpublished when he wrote. But he perfects our knowledge admirably in many cases, especially concerning Paul. On the whole, this oldest Church history, for those who read it rightly, is indispensable to the proper understanding of the Apostolic period.

* * *

We need not say much about the historical value of the Pauline letters. As the self-evidence of the great Apostolic missionary they are the classical sources for the events of his life and for the appreciation of his inner life. In addition, they throw important light on the historical figure of Jesus, and by means of a great number of separate pictures they illuminate the external and the internal life of

Apostolic Christianity. Whoever merely estimates these letters as documents of the Imperial period will receive much profit. So far as I can see there is no such wealth of spiritual self-evidence of any other man of the Imperial period.

In all these directions the historical value of the letters of Paul is particularly high because of the fact which I have often emphasized that they are unliterary texts. Paul never thought when he dictated these letters that they would be published, and as published texts would become part of a Holy Book and of the literature of the world. He could not think of a future in which they would be read and criticized. According to his belief there would be no long future. Therefore there was no need for him to pose for posterity. Rather he expressed the moods and the thoughts which arose from the particular circumstances.

The other relics we possess from the Apostolic period have also their great historical value, because they reflect clearly the early Christian piety in the rich variety of its personalities; almost like a volcano eruption as in the Revelation of John, again calmed and consolidated in the Catholic Epistles, then shortly seeking expression in technical theological terms, as in the Epistle to the Hebrews.

* * *

Let us look back. The historical value of the New Testament as a whole lies in the fact that it gives us a fragmentary yet trustworthy knowledge of the personalities of Jesus and Paul, and of the essence and nature of Early Christianity. This information is not given in fixed formulas but in thousands of occasional intimations, which the historian must often cut loose from their connections, which are to him accidental, in the manifold strata of their historical transmission.

The new method of working which considers the New Testament in the clearest light of its period, of its Eastern home, and its social class, has altered the judgments on the historical value of the New Testament in many details, but on the whole confirmed its historical value, because it clamped the Holy Book to its contemporary world. The New Testament does not hover without historical connection above its period, but is bound to it by innumerable ties. It spoke the language of its native Mediterranean world. It grew entwined in the class where Christianity originated. It is the reliable residue of the spiritual movement, which refers back to one center of spiritual force, Jesus Christ.

* * *

That which we call in history "reliable" has never, it is true, the character of unconditional finality or of mathematical precision. Every historical result is relative. And consequently there is no lack of whimsical excess of historical imagination, which cannot be controlled by automatic means. In most cases, and especially with the great problems of the spiritual history of mankind, the historian has no absolute final method and can give no conclusive proof. He often works with hypotheses, and with all striving for accuracy and objectivity his work is still tainted with an unavoidable subjective element.

But the partaker in this historical work knows well that in spite of all subjectivity and other human failures, historical knowledge progresses, slowly, it is true, but irresistibly toward the truth. Therefore he is not alarmed when the subjectivity of the investigator or the imagination of the dilettante fancy that they can pilfer the ancient riches of mankind from the treasure house of the centuries and substitute miserable tinsel for gold. It seems that Clio, the Muse of History, after the hard day's work of her followers needs the game of the fantastic, which she views with a motherly smile.

* * *

More than two hundred years ago the French Jesuit, Jean Hardouin, defended with all seriousness the thesis that the whole of the ancient literature in the Greek and Latin languages with the exception of the works of Homer, Herodotus, Cicero, the Georgics of Virgil, the satires and epistles of Horace, the work of the elder Pliny, and a few other texts, was the work of monks in the Thirteenth Century A. D., under the direction of a certain Severus Archontius. It was the same Hardouin who, in 1715, published a work of twelve volumes on the Christian Councils from the year 34 to 1714, although he maintained that all Councils before the Tridentine were not historical. When asked why he had written their history he said: "That is not known to anybody except God and myself." After the impassionate war of pens which arose over the radical theses of this man, nothing remained except a sarcastic epitaph; Jacob Vernet of Geneva, who had, perhaps, noticed that smile of Clio, wrote it:

"*in expectatione indicii hic iacet hominum paradoxotatus . . . credulitate puer, audacia iuvenis, deliriis senex,*"

"Here lies, waiting the last judgment, the

most paradoxical of all men, in his credulity a child, in his audacity a youth, in his delirious mind an old man."

In the year 1841 a scholar named Kirschbaum, reviving an old hypothesis, seriously maintained the view that the work of the Jew, Philo of Alexandria, was a forgery of Christian men of literature of the Second Century A. D. Thirty years ago the Aramaic papyri of the Fifth Century B. C. from Elephantine came to light. It was an epoch-making discovery for Jewish history, and the sheets are to-day among the most valuable treasures of our European museums. In 1909, during the exultations of orientalists and historians, a dissonant voice was heard which declared these original sheets to be absolute forgeries.

We need no more examples. Whoever is in touch with historical research knows that historical investigation does not tyrannize a man by compelling him to accept its results.

There will always be some people whose eyes

are so made that they cannot observe a thing without, I may say, observing it to pieces.

It would be wrong if we had no more than mockery and ridicule for these blighted eyes and pilfering hands. I mean that we should allow no place for mockery and ridicule where we, in bad mistakes, find honest striving for historical knowledge. We should leave history itself to announce the judgment. When the time has come that motherly smile will flash over Clio's pensive face.

* * *

It is now more than twenty years since, one afternoon in spring, as the sun was sinking, I rode on the Ionian coast coming from Miletus toward an ancient Anatolian sanctuary, the ruins of the temple of Apollo at Didyma. On the right was the Ægean Sea with the bare rocks of the distant islands of Samos, Patmos, and Cos. In front Didyma was gradually appearing, a heap of marble and ruins out of which arose the three massive columns of the ancient temple glistening in the evening sun.

Long ago a desired object of the archæological treasure digger, this temple of Apollo at Didyma, destroyed by earthquakes and the storms of centuries, had to suffer blasting with dynamite, at the hands of men.

But the foundations of the temple withstood the dynamite. They withstood it because they lay huge and massive, deep in the earth. The earthquakes had been able to destroy the columns; the foundations survived both history and barbarous force.

The foundations of our historical knowledge of Early Christianity taken as a whole seem to me unassailable. Although hidden to those eyes which cannot see into the depths, they lie huge and massive and imperishable in the depth.

VI

THE RELIGIOUS VALUE OF THE NEW TESTAMENT

IV

THE RELIGIOUS VALUE OF THE NEW
TESTAMENT

VI

THE RELIGIOUS VALUE OF THE NEW TESTAMENT

THE question of the religious value of the New Testament is not nearly so difficult to answer as the question of its historical value. Everything religious is simple. It becomes complicated only when strange elements are introduced into it.

This question as to the religious value can only be answered from a religious standpoint. A work of art cannot be appreciated by a savage, and the religious value of the New Testament cannot be appreciated by a man who has no feeling for religion. Just as the grinning savage would perhaps shatter the work of art with a blow of his club, so the unreligious man would regard as absurd the question of the religious value of the New Testament.

Thus the religious value of the New Testament cannot be forced upon anyone by demonstrations. It can only be perceived by the man who has a sensitiveness for the sublime object. It obtrudes itself upon the religious man.

Therefore there is no need for long words to prove that value. It is written large on every page of the New Testament. But it is advisable first of all to avert a misunderstanding which, I believe, is still widespread. I have already touched upon it in the fifth lecture.

* * *

Many believe that the religious value of a Biblical text depends on the results of historical criticism. As a young theologian I shared this opinion. But I came to regard it more and more as untenable. With the final rejection of that principle, I experienced a beneficent inner deliverance.

I was of the opinion that the demonstration of the historical value of the New Testament was the basis for the recognition and validity of its religious value. I thought that theological science must for each new generation, perhaps with new methods, first bring the demonstration of the historical value of the classical sources of the New Testament, and that on this foundation would arise the religious value and the religious appreciation of the New Testament would be possible, beginning with personal edification and going on to the edification of communities and inspiration of the work of evangelization and missions. Put in other words, if the demonstration of the historical value of the classical sources should fail, as a whole or in part, through a proof of the spuriousness of any one of the texts, then the religious foundation not only of the Christian Church but also of Christianity in general would be shaken.

This theory to which I look back to-day with sympathy as belonging to struggling youth, expressed in formula would be this: the historical is the basis of the holy. Whoever understands this formula in all that it implies will perceive that with it an attitude is taken to one of the greatest problems of modern thought since the time of Richard Simon, Spinoza, and Lessing. It is a problem, recognized or not, that lies behind all controversies about the Bible which have moved and shaken, impoverished and enriched, Christendom since historical criticism entered into theology.

I cannot unfold at full length this problem of the relation of the historical to the holy. I must be content with emphasizing that I became more and more convinced of the primacy and the autonomy of the holy. A very great part of the historical flows directly or indirectly from the self-manifestation of the holy, while the holy has many inner relations with the historical. But finally the holy depends on itself, and in itself lies the source of its immanent development. The holy is prehistoric and metahistoric. The holy does not live on the favors of history. It lives on the secret of divine spontaneous generation.

That we value the New Testament as Holy Scriptures thus need not be justified on the detour of a historical examination of its contents, because it is justified from within through the testimony which our fathers called the "*testimonium spiritus Sancti internum*," "the testimony of the Holy Spirit from within," and which Paul called the "demonstration of the Spirit and of power" (I Cor. 2:4). Our examination of the historical value of the New Testament, therefore, did not mean that we sought to find in a secular way something that was necessary in the interest of the holy, like a foundation of hewn stones on which the *Sanctissimum* could be erected. It did not mean that in the laboratory of the week-day we sought to distill the Water of Life for Sunday, or that the New Testament chair should be the fire protection for the pulpit.

With these main indications I profess a conception of religion which is more mystic and practical than intellectual. Religion, and especially Christian religion, does not consist for me in the first place in acknowledging certain facts of the past. Christian religion is to me a living and moving in the present living God, a fellowship with the living Christ, which is a fellowship of submission and of following Him. The facts of the past have an eminent religious value, but they acquire that value from our present faith. The facts of the past are not the basis of faith. The only basis of our faith is the present living God, and Jesus Christ when He has become for us in some way or other a present and effective Reality. We will also, it is true, welcome thankfully the result of the historical examination of the New Testament for its religious valuation. It is of the greatest importance for all of us, for theologians and for the churches, to know that we have in the New Testament an excellent historical tradition of Jesus and His Apostles.

But to know the past is not the unconditional basis for our present-day living in the higher world.

* * *

It is in connection with this that I now raise the question, whether the title of our lecture is correctly formulated. Would it not be more accurate, instead of speaking of the religious value of the New Testament, to speak of the value of the religion of Early Christianity? Certainly it was not the influence of the written New Testament which worked historically in the missions of the first centuries. The New Testament was not then collected, but was yet to be formed. The influence was that of the holy Christian personalities in whom primitive Christianity was embodied. The New Testament, as such, is the reflection of Early Christianity. It is the residue of a powerful religious movement which long had been active. Certainly the New Testament was not the basis of Early Christianity: "The foundation is laid, namely Jesus Christ, and no one can lay another" (I Cor. 3:11).

But for the purpose of study as well as of our personal religious attitude we cannot grasp primitive Christianity historically as well as religiously except in the self-evidence which has been preserved in the New Testament. It follows that in this lecture "The Religion of the New Testament" means the same, at least in a certain sense, as "the religion of Early Christianity."

It is true that if the religion of Early Christianity is to be understood historically it must be considered in its historical development from the Old Testament up to Jesus and from Jesus to Paul and John, and all from the background of contemporary religion and culture. It must be considered as a "movement," as something that grows and as something that changes, as a particular case of historical undulation. But in our practical theme we have to consider it as something which has become calm, as something complete, as something which has reached a great synthesis in the New Testament, as something present to us to-day as revelation.

* * *

We must continue with critical remarks. The historical study of the New Testament did not always make easy the historical approach to New Testament Religion. Many scholars never pronounced the subject, "The Religion of the New Testament," with the emphasis on the word "religion." Moreover, they did not even formulate the theme, "The Religion of the New Testament," at all. There are innumerable works which deal with the "theology" of the New Testament, but a generation ago there was hardly a single European work which dealt with the "religion" of the New Testament. It was quite a surprise to me when, about twenty years ago, a book appeared with this title, written by my honored predecessor in Berlin, Dr. Bernhard Weiss, who had already published a big *Theology of the New Testament*. It is only during the last decades that the historical problem of the religion of the New Testament has been raised.

How is the fact to be explained that so little was said about the Religion of the New Testament in the theological literature of the past? I can only answer with a confession of the guilt of my own science. It is because we have, for one-sided doctrinaire interests, strained our eyes with doctrinaire matters, until, unfortunately, we became too often religion-blind.

According to this statement it is obviously presupposed that theology is something different from religion. By this I am continuing the hints which I gave before.

What, then, is the difference between religion and theology?

Religion, in any form, is a practical relation with a superhuman, divine power. Theology is scientific reflection on religion. It makes an historical investigation into the phenomena of religious life in the history of mankind. Besides this relatively recent function it has also long undertaken speculative and normative tasks. But it is the science of religion, not religion itself. Religion and theology are related to each other in the same way as art and the science of art, law and the science of law, language and the science of language, the starry heaven and astronomy. Theology is secondary, religion is primary. Theology is the scientific reflection upon the phenomena of personal life, religion *is* the personal life depending on God.

Thus when we inquire into the religion of Early Christianity as it is reflected in the New Testament, we inquire into religious, spiritual realities, and not into theological teaching or systems.

The teaching and the system are only possible when preceded by the life. Whoever inquires about the theology of the New Testament and not about its religion, deals with its secondary derivative aspects instead of the powerful, living, primary facts.

* * *

At the very beginning this method leads itself into a maze. At the beginning stands Jesus. And if anything can be said of Him with certainty, it is this: He was not a theologian. He was quite untheological, neither did He speak "like the scribes" (Matt. 7:29).

Jesus is all religion, all life; He is not a book or a system. He is Spirit and Fire. To speak of the theology of Jesus is a triviality. He had no theology, for He had the living God. And His revelations, His words of comfort and His exhortations, are witnesses to His possession. Whoever undertakes to put together a theology of Jesus from His confessions makes a blossoming field into an herbarium. Let us, then, when investigating the New Testament historically and valuing it religiously, leave the "theology" of Jesus alone. It exists only in the gloomy shadows of modern books. It has never existed in the light of day, and not a single soul in the ancient world was moved, nor would anyone to-day be moved, by the "theology" of Jesus.

But how is it then with Paul? It is true that Paul, as a pupil of the Rabbi Gamaliel, had become something of a theologian. But when we call him the great theologian of Early Christianity it is questionable whether we have grasped his characteristic features. I say that we have not. Also in the case of the Apostle of Jesus Christ, religion is primary, not only when we regard him during his psychological development, but also when he is the mature Paul. Paul is the prophet and the missionary of Early Christianity. It is true, he was not the creator but the organizer of the cult of Jesus Christ. But he lived in Christ. He is the deepest Christ mystic of the early period. One can, and indeed one must, speak of a theology of Paul. But it is wrong not to speak, first of all, of his religion, which glows and works underneath the surface even of the more theological parts of his letters. Therefore, as historians and as believers, we refuse to make a Paulinism out of Paul, to make a lifeless system out of a man. The religion of

Paul has been, and is to-day, of far greater influence than his theology; his fellowship with Christ far more than his Christology.

And that is the atmosphere of Early Christianity generally. It is true that, soon after the time of Paul, Early Christianity set out distinctly on the path of theology. The Epistle to the Hebrews, as we saw before, is the first classical example. It is predominantly a theological treatise and demonstration. From that time on the whole history of the ancient Church is not only the history of striving to become an organized body but also of the theological development of Christianity.

But Early Christianity exercised its great influence as a religion, as divine power, which was transmitted by personal contact, as inner life from man to man, from conscience to conscience. And afterward, during the ages, the most powerful periods of Christianity have always been the religious periods. The Reformation has been a reformation because it had a religious soul. Where, in the history of the Church, theology has taken the first place, she clipped the wings of those who would ascend to the clouds like an eagle. She often made men timid, distrustful of each other, and unbrotherly. She destroyed unity and bred the sectarian spirit. Where, on the other hand, theology has accomplished something great in history, it has only been possible through the living force of great religious personalities.

The assertion that in Early Christianity and in the New Testament theology is predominant can only be made by that doctrinairism which is also guilty of those other errors which I have pointed out during these lectures: those theories that the letters of Paul are literary works, that the Gospels are art prose, and that the New Testament Greek is to be isolated as something exceptional in the study of language. It was this doctrinairism which also dragged Early Christianity as a theological movement into the spheres of those "isms" of ancient philosophical reflection and speculation. Having no appreciation for life and originality, it made the confessions of saintly and struggling men into paragraphs, and thought it could put the Saviour and His Apostle in the strait-jacket of a system.

If we wish to understand historically and to value personally the religion of the New Testament, then we must come down from the sphere of literary culture, which was not the sphere of Early Christianity, to the level of non-literary humanity. And if we are trained to study the lines which came from the midst of those people they will give us a great help in attaining a complete understanding of the religious character of Early Christianity, because they will give us a better grasp of the nature of naïve sentiment, of non-theological religion, of pre-dogmatic surrender to the ever-present deity.

I said before that to know the past is not the unconditional basis for our present-day living in the eternal world. And it is not the unconditional basis for the present-day personal valuation of the New Testament. There are many Christians, men as well as women, who, without any training in historical methods, are able to value the New Testament from within excellently. But, of course, the external historical understanding of the religious, pre-dogmatical character of the New Testament is a help for the approach to its religious valuation.

* * *

Now this question as to its real religious value is answered by the New Testament from within to the religious man in different ways. In the religious valuation of the New Testament there are strong subjective gradations. But all who hear that *testimonium internum* will be one in their confession: here speaks the living God, here speaks the living Christ. This must be learned better by all of us, to flee from the often uncontrollable past of mankind's history to the present God.

The standpoint which I have here indicated seems to me to be of exceptional importance when we deal with the separate questions of our theme, especially with one of the greatest of them: the question of the religious value of the Johannine texts, and the Johannine Gospel in particular. As a source of pure historical information the Johannine Gospel stands behind the Synoptic Gospels. But that does not prejudice its religious value. It is just this Gospel with its indifference to minute historical records that painted the ever-present Christ before the eyes of the community. It reveals to us, as likewise the Johannine letters, the Living One who *is* the Spirit, who *is* the Word, who *is* the Paraclete with the Father, who *is* the Vine and we its branches. There stands forth He who *is* the Shepherd, He who *is* the Door, He who *is* the lasting atonement for our sins.

The Johannine Gospel, in which Christ always says emphatically, "I am," does not reveal the Christ who *has been* the Word, Spirit, Vine, and Shepherd in the past, but the Christ who is the Word, Spirit, Vine, and Shepherd to-day. And when the Gospel of John says, using the imperfect, "In the beginning *was* the Word," it does not mean something completed in the *past*, but the eternal coming of Christ from the beginning, revealing the eternal, living God. It is this powerful, vibrating conviction running through the Johannine letters which constitutes the religious value of the Johannine writings, and not their biographical details. It is from this conviction that the facts of the past receive their divine light, and in particular the Cross receives its light by the exalted Christ. The piety of Paul, culminating in the fellowship with the exalted Lord, has become a completed whole in the Johannine Gospel and has created definite cult forms of expression for itself, in which the believers from that time onward could render their confessions to the glorified Master.

* * *

I have put these remarks on the Johannine writings first because I believe that this part of the New Testament in the light of modern study presents perhaps the greatest difficulties to earnest Christians.

The difficulties with regard to the Synoptic Gospels are much fewer because they reveal the Master's personality much more distinctly than the great confession book of the Johannine Gospel desired to do. The Johannine Gospel shows to us the Word which has again become Spirit, the Synoptic Gospels show more the Word which has become flesh. That vein of gold of which we spoke when dealing with the different strata of the Synoptic tradition during our examination of their historical value, the golden vein of the sayings of Jesus, is also decisive for the religious valuation of the Synoptic Gospels. But it must be clear at this point that the religious valuation does not begin with asking, "What did Jesus, who once lived in Palestine under Tiberius and Pontius Pilate, say?" The question of the religious value is much more of this nature, "What does Jesus command of me to-day, what does He expect from His Church

RELIGIOUS VALUE

to-day? What goal does He set to-day for the work of the social classes, of the peoples, of mankind?" If the great German poet-philosopher, Friedrich Nietzsche, wrote above one of his great works, "Thus said Zarathustra," we can write under the Synoptic Gospels, valuing them as revelation, the words "Thus says Jesus," "Thus says Jesus to-day," "Thus He speaks to me and to all of us to-day."

Putting the question in that form, we cannot expect the words of Jesus which move mankind to have everywhere the same effect as if they operated mechanically. Because the question of religious value will be asked by individual men, the answers will be different on account of the subjective element. There are words of Jesus which say little or nothing to a young man who is not yet troubled by the great problems of life, but which have a great deal to say to the fighter struggling with the powers of darkness, or to the patient woman who knows no rest from the day's cares. There are words of Jesus which retreat at one period in order to appear to the following generation like a cherub with a flaming sword, or like a messenger of peace from the heavenly Jerusalem. But there is not a single word of Jesus which can in no place and at no time be a divine revelation for a man.

We need not prove this revealing character of the words of the Master with our theological arts, or with the subtlety of our academic apologetics. Jesus justifies Himself—justifies Himself wherever He wishes. There is no secret code, no *nova lex* in those words which were never written by His hand. In those words which are always bursting the husk of the letter in which they are inclosed to-day the soul of Jesus breathes—the immortal, the eternal soul of Jesus. In these words is revealed to-day the will of Jesus, the eternal will of Jesus which is the will of the Father. From these words there streams to-day the power for regeneration and the hopeful waiting for the coming of the Kingdom of God.

The Synoptic words of Jesus have still another religious value: they remain for us the backbone of Pauline and Johannine Christianity which is adopted in church worship. They preserve this Cult-Christianity, this deep mystical Christianity from sentimental weakening, from doctrinaire dissipation and hardening, as well as from gnostic exaggerations of imagination. They give to the ecclesiastical Pauline-Johannine Christianity its support, its norm, and, when necessary, its correction.

* * *

Just as simple as in the case of the Synoptic Gospels is the question of the religious value of the Pauline letters. It will appear more so to the degree the non-literary character of the letters is recognized also in religious consideration. The Pauline letters are not the cold, black rock of a lava stream which has been petrified for centuries; rather we find ourselves here in the vicinity of an ever-active volcano. His Christ enthusiasm emits warm rays of light which warm our hearts when they are cold, so that thus our sealed souls open to admit Christ Himself. That is also true with different degrees of energy in the other Apostolic writings.

* * *

After all, the religious value of the New Testament is contained in this: that this little book brings us into sure contact with our Lord Jesus Christ and His first witnesses.

And this contact with Jesus and with His disciples means fellowship with the living God, means a steady hope for the Kingdom of God and of eternal life, it means forgiveness of sin and salvation, triumph in the midst of affliction, power and help for all good, moral earnestness, self-denial, brotherliness, unity.

Considered historically, the New Testament is the trustworthy record of Jesus and His Apostles. Religiously considered, it proves itself from within by its influence to be the Magna Charta of the present Jesus Christ.

Therefore we confess the New Testament as a Holy Book, the Book of Life. And we are confident that the New Testament, in virtue of its own unique power, as it enters more into the clear light of modern investigation and as it penetrates further among men of all races and tongues, will justify the judgment that it is both: the trustworthy record of the beginning of our religion, and the Magna Charta of the present Jesus Christ.

www.ingramcontent.com/pod-product-compliance
Lightning Source LLC
Chambersburg PA
CBHW051925160426
43198CB00012B/2043